The
Culture
of
Contentment

RECENT BOOKS BY
JOHN KENNETH GALBRAITH

Economics in Perspective:
A Critical History

A Tenured Professor

The
Culture
of
Contentment

John Kenneth Galbraith

SINCLAIR-STEVENSON LTD

First published in Great Britain by
Sinclair-Stevenson
7/8 Kendrick Mews
London SW7 3HG

Copyright © 1992 by John Kenneth Galbraith

Reprinted 1992

First published in the United States in 1992 by
Houghton Mifflin Company.

British Library Cataloguing in Publication Data
A CIP catalogue record for this book is available from the British
Library.

ISBN: 1 85619 147 8

Book design by Robert Overholtzer

Printed in England by Clays Ltd, St Ives plc.

To Kitty
once more with love

A Word of Thanks

As ever, I am in the debt of the friends and associates who make my books possible and the writing of them — and, one hopes, the reading — endurable. I have especially in mind colleagues and friends at Harvard and indeed also, as it is known on this side of the Atlantic, the other Cambridge. With them over the months and years I have discussed and sometimes, without doubt, appropriated ideas that are here offered or elaborated.

More specifically, my son James Galbraith, professor of economics at the University of Texas, helped me, and notably, on matters of factual detail. Nan Bers typed and retyped the manuscript with good humor and, considering my handwriting, surprising accuracy; as I've often told, the note of spontaneity that my critics say they admire so much appears only in the fifth draft. Edith Tucker, a friend of many years, checked for factual errors, although any that remain are surely mine. Sue Carlson ably held off phone calls and intruders in the last days before press and publication.

To no one, however, am I so indebted, and as so often

before, as to my editor and partner in both management and composition, Andrea Williams. Without her efforts, which some, to be sure, will regret, there would have been no book. To her my great and enduring thanks.

Finally, needless to say, the requisite room in my life for this writing has been made by Catherine Atwater Galbraith, from whom also has come unfailing support over long days, weeks and months. To her, not for the first time, I dedicate a book.

John Kenneth Galbraith
Cambridge, Massachusetts

Contents

1. The Culture of Contentment   1
2. The Social Character of Contentment: 13
   An Overview
3. The Functional Underclass   30
4. Taxation and the Public Services: 42
   The Perverse Effect
5. The License for Financial Devastation   51
6. The Bureaucratic Syndrome   65
7. The Economic Accommodation, I   78
8. The Economic Accommodation, II   95
9. The Foreign Policy of Contentment: 109
   The Recreational and the Real
10. The Military Nexus, I   122
11. The Military Nexus, II   133
12. The Politics of Contentment   144
13. The Reckoning, I   154
14. The Reckoning, II   166
15. Requiem   174
    Index   185

The
Culture
of
Contentment

1

The Culture of Contentment

THE LESSONS OF HISTORY are not to be taken too readily or without question. Life, in particular economic life, is in a constant process of change, and, in consequence, the same action or event occurring at different times can lead to very different results. The stock market crash of October 1929 shattered, or initiated the shattering of, a fragile banking, investment and general economic structure in the United States, and there followed the long and rigorously painful experience of the Great Depression. In 1987, a similar, no less traumatic break in the market in the financially unfortunate month of October had a less devastating economic result. Built into the American economy in the fifty-eight-year interim had been an array of public measures — insurance of bank and notably of savings and loan deposits, welfare payments, unemployment compensation, old-age pensions, support to farm prices, an implicit public commitment that allows no really large enterprise, banking or industrial, to fail — that had given it an economically and socially rewarding resilience.

I

There are, however, some lessons in a larger frame that do endure. The most nearly invariant is that individuals and communities that are favored in their economic, social and political condition attribute social virtue and political durability to that which they themselves enjoy. That attribution, in turn, is made to apply even in the face of commanding evidence to the contrary. The beliefs of the fortunate are brought to serve the cause of continuing contentment, and the economic and political ideas of the time are similarly accommodated. There is an eager political market for that which pleases and reassures. Those who would serve this market and reap the resulting reward in money and applause are reliably available.

Thus it was in Rome after Trajan, when the Empire went visibly on the defensive. Life in Rome itself showed no sign of accepting the weakness so evident on the frontiers — the terrible new fact that in the Empire, as would be the case with imperial rule so often again, it was now thought better to be without than within. Certainly much later there were few doubts among the happily privileged, strongly self-approving, if hygienically deprived, throng that surrounded and sustained Louis XV, Louis XVI and Marie Antoinette in Paris and out at Versailles. A forceful set of economic ideas, those of the Physiocrats, affirmed the principles by which those so favored were rewarded. These ideas supported and celebrated an economic system that returned all wealth, superficial deductions for trade and manufacturing apart, to the owners of the land, the aristocrats who inhabited and served the Court.

The case continues. The great entrepreneurs and their acolytes who were dominant in British, German, French and then American political and economic life in the nineteenth century and on into the early decades of the twentieth were not in doubt as to their economic and social destiny, and this, again, was duly affirmed by the companion views of the classical economists. One could not feel guilt-stricken about one's good fortune given a working class that, according to Ricardo and Malthus, relentlessly bred itself down to subsistence levels, or when one was oneself subject to a market system that rewarded effort in accordance with specific economic contribution and larger social merit.

By the early decades of this century the alienation and anger generated by these attitudes and the resulting economic hardship and abuse were for all to see. In Britain steps by Chancellor of the Exchequer Lloyd George to ameliorate the situation through taxation, medical assistance to the helpless and especially compensation for the unemployed produced violent resistance on the part of the contented — in 1910–11, a constitutional crisis, two elections and perhaps the greatest parliamentary convulsion since Oliver Cromwell. It is now widely agreed that the measures then so opposed by the fortunate saved British capitalism in the particularly grim years following World War I.

The circumstances were the same a little later in the United States, where by 1932 the Great Depression, widespread uncompensated unemployment, farm disasters, old age without succoring income, resistance to trade unions and factory abuse of women and children had induced doubt as to whether the American economic system could or, indeed, should survive. The country was a simmering cauldron of discontent. Those still favored were, however, far from concerned and again far from disposed to accept the economic action by which they might be saved. So strong was their voice that Franklin D. Roosevelt was elected to his first term by a species of political deception. While promising change, economic revival and reform, he reassured those in deeply satisfied opposition by promising also the balanced budget and reduced public expenditure that would effectively ensure that nothing much would be different. George Bush was not the first presidential candidate whose lips had to be read with some attention.

The later reaction of the comfortable and contented to the Roosevelt reforms — the New Deal — is part of American history. The affluent and otherwise well-situated cited, initially, the constitutional barriers to the necessarily enhanced federal intervention in the economy, a matter on which for most of Roosevelt's first two terms they had the support of a socially contented and thus sympathetic judiciary.

There was also powerful opposition on economic grounds, and for this the voices of influential economists were amply available. Joseph Alois Schumpeter, a figure of world reputation then at Harvard, and the only slightly less noted Lionel Robbins of the London School of Economics united in arguing that recovery could not and should not come by government action. Depression and all its discomforts were necessary to extrude the poison from the economic system. "Our analysis," Schumpeter, speaking collectively, averred, "leads us to believe that recovery is sound only if it does come of itself."[1] Edwin W. Kemmerer of Princeton, the most celebrated monetarist of his time, rallied his coreligionists into the Economists' National Committee on Monetary Policy to resist the administration's not implausible efforts to reverse deflation by abandoning fixed-price convertibility of the dollar into gold.

There were also, of course, economists in support of the innovative and protective policies of the administration: Rexford Guy Tugwell, Lauchlin Currie, Harry Dexter White, Leon Henderson, Adolf Berle (who was, by training though not by inclination, a lawyer), Gardiner C. Means and others, but they are seen in the histories of the time as exceptional, often courageous, sometimes deviant figures who rejected the established orthodoxy of the age.

Considered socially more reputable was the opposition that did not attempt to disguise or evade the reality of contentment. Testifying before a Senate committee, the American banker J. P. Morgan warned, "If you destroy

---

1. "Depressions," in *The Economics of the Recovery Program* (New York: Whittlesey House, McGraw-Hill, 1934), p. 20. A similar observation by Lionel Robbins is in *The Great Depression* (London: Macmillan, 1934).

the leisure class, you destroy civilization." Asked later by reporters to identify the leisure class, he said, "All those who can afford to hire a maid."[2] For Morgan the threat from Washington was no casual concern: "The family of J. P. Morgan used to warn visitors against mentioning Roosevelt's name in [his] august presence lest fury raise his blood pressure to the danger point."[3]

It is now generally accepted that the Roosevelt revolution saved the traditional capitalist economic system in the United States and the well-being of those whom capitalism most favored. By adaptation the anger and alienation were diminished, and economic life became more stable and secure. This would not have happened had those who, in the full maturity of time, were saved and most rewarded had their way. If in the election of 1932 they had been fully aware of what was to come, there might well have been no salvation. The energy, money, public concern and propaganda that would have been released in that year by a full knowledge of the impending changes could well have assured a Roosevelt defeat.

The larger point is not in doubt: the fortunate and the favored, it is more than evident, do not contemplate and respond to their own longer-run well-being. Rather, they respond, and powerfully, to immediate comfort and contentment. This is the controlling mood. And this is

2. Quoted in Arthur M. Schlesinger, Jr., *The Coming of the New Deal*, vol. 2 of *The Age of Roosevelt* (Boston: Houghton Mifflin, 1958), p. 479.
3. Schlesinger, p. 567.

so not only in the capitalist world, as it is still called; a deeper and more general human instinct is here involved.

There was a time in the Soviet Union and, if in lesser measure, in the countries under Communist domination after World War II when comprehensive socialism — the social ownership of all productive resources and the associated political constraint and control — was far from unwelcome. It was in agreeable contrast with the remnants of feudalism and the purposeless rulers — the Czars in Russia, later Horthy in Hungary, Pilsudski and his successors in Poland and other narrow, reactionary and feckless leaders — who had been replaced by revolution. The planning and command system of socialism worked very well for building transport, electrical utility, steel and other basic industries, and in the Soviet Union the huge weapons industry that turned back the armies of Adolf Hitler and then challenged in space and other technology the United States itself.

The system failed because it did not serve efficiently for agriculture in those countries where socialism extended to that recalcitrant industry and to the marketing of farm products. Agriculture works well only under a widely accepted and much celebrated form of exploitation, that by the farmer of himself, his family and his immediate and loyal hired hands. The system also could not satisfy the infinitely diverse and unstable demand for the services and products that make up the modern consumers' goods economy. Here socialism, both in planning and administration, proved far too inflexible. One may marvel at the attraction of often frivolous and dispensable consumer artifacts and entertainments in our time, but their ultimately controlling appeal cannot be doubted.

There was another, more grievous source of failure. That was in not recognizing that even the most modest economic advance brings into existence more diversely educated and motivated people than, as a practical matter, can be kept quiet and thus excluded from the institutions by which they are governed. This is true in all the industrial countries without exception.

A poor peasantry, scattered over the landscape, working from dawn to dusk in order to live, can, with a little effort, be controlled and politically disenfranchised. For accomplishing this, there is the amply available assistance of the landlords. The vast and functionally inevitable contingent of scientists, journalists, professors, artists, poets, self-anointed saviors of the public soul and students — especially students — all of them seeking and then demanding participation in the modern industrial society, cannot be similarly manipulated. Freedom of expression and public participation in government are widely heralded as social virtues; it is too little noticed that beyond a certain point in economic development they become socially necessary and politically inescapable.

So it was in Poland, Czechoslovakia, Hungary, Bulgaria and East Germany before the explosion of the autumn and winter of 1989–90. So, over a longer time, it was in the USSR. In all these countries a favored Communist elite was taken by surprise.

Evidence of mass dissatisfaction was almost certainly available. There were secret police to inform on such matters, and while liberty has anciently been served by police incompetence, that has its limits. In some of these countries — East Germany, Czechoslovakia, Hungary — television told of the living standards, the consumer enjoyments (and frivolities) in neighboring Austria and West Germany. Similar strong word came from the United States. There was obvious question as to why they were denied at home.

To the old leaders, however, and those in prestigious association therewith there was the comfort of convenient belief. They were protected in their fortunate position by the presumed power of socialist principles, adherence to which assured survival. They were in the great and immutable current of history identified for all time by Marx and Lenin. It was agreed that the transition, admittedly gradual, to the ultimate and benign world of complete Communism would require their own interim exercise of power — the dictatorship of the proletariat, also called by them the democracy of the masses. This authority those in power could not but suppose was accepted. Thus, to repeat, was belief accommodated to the need and comfort of the favored. So it was until the day when the crowds flooded into the streets and showed, not to the surprise of the old leaders alone, that if the numbers are great enough, no armed response is serviceable. This took place first in Eastern Europe and then, in the late summer days of 1991, in the Soviet Union.

Few things in very recent times could have been further from accepted and proclaimed thought than the possibility that the explosive events in Eastern Europe could have a parallel in the United States or perhaps in Britain. Communism had failed; capitalism was triumphant. Could anyone be so dour, so pessimistic, as to suggest that lurking in the successful system and in its larger and well-proclaimed democracy were grave flaws similarly concealed by preferred belief? Alas, there are. But the power of contentment over belief is universal; it extends alike over time and space. It is not confined by the comparative trivia of ideology; it affects all.

What *is* new in the so-called capitalist countries — and this is a vital point — is that the controlling contentment and resulting belief is now that of the many, not just of the few. It operates under the compelling cover of democracy, albeit a democracy not of all citizens but of those who, in defense of their social and economic advantage, actually go to the polls. The result is government that is accommodated not to reality or common need but to the beliefs of the contented, who are now the majority of those who vote. A consensus old as democratic government itself still prevails.

A word needs to be added on the mood in which one writes a book such as this. That mood must be analytical and not adjuratory, detached and not, so far as possible, politically involved. Presidents or lesser politicians, individually or collectively, can be advised and, when appropriate, condemned. So can those who offer them advice and guidance. But this is not true of a community such as that with which I am here concerned. Its nature and public tendency can be described and analyzed. The consequences of its actions may be unfortunate and regrettable, as is here shown frequently to be the case, but the people responsible cannot be condemned; a whole community cannot usefully be blamed or excoriated.

The author of an essay such as this must, in some measure, use the method of the anthropologist, not that of the economist or the political theorist. Examining the tribal rites of strange and different peoples, those, say, of a distant island in Polynesia, the scholar finds practices and ceremonials that, on occasion, seem personally distasteful and sometimes socially abhorrent. They are to be observed but not censured; one does not effectively censure an established pattern of life.

This is the case with the political economy of contentment with which I here deal. It is a culture that is of intense interest and importance, or so obviously I would choose to believe. Thus the need for studying and understanding it. But it is not a proper subject for indignation nor is it one in which reform can be seriously expected. As the anthropologist does not attack the extravagant sexual rites, severe self-mutilation and occasional self-immolation of the culture he has under examination and does not expect it to change, that, at least in some measure, must be the attitude here.

This is perhaps especially to be urged in my case as the author. I have lived nearly all of my life in the world of self-approving contentment. As to the rewards accruing to that community, I am, in a personal way, without complaint. That this association, indeed identity, contributes to my understanding I would obviously like to think. But just as firmly it warns me against the usefulness of criticism and certainly about the value of injunctions to reform. It is the nature of contentment that it resists that which invades it with vigor and often, as in very recent times, with strongly voiced indignation. This too I have learned from long and intimate association. Were I not personally aware of, even experienced in, the ethos of contentment and its highly motivated resistance to change and reform, there would be valid doubt as to my qualification for writing this book.

2

The Social Character
of Contentment

AN OVERVIEW

IN THE UNITED STATES in recent years highly relevant attention in literary and political expression has
been accorded the dismaying number of individuals
and families that are very poor. In 1989, in the United
States, 12.8 percent of the population, young and old, lived
below the poverty line of $12,674 for a family of four, the
largest number of them belonging to minority groups.
There are severe social, law enforcement, drug, housing
and health problems that come from the concentration
of these unfortunates in the inner cities and, if less visibly,
in the declining or defunct mining, manufacturing and
agricultural areas, notably on the Appalachian plateau,
the once populous low mountain range that stands back
of the eastern seaboard, and on the poor farms of the Deep
South.

The much larger number of Americans who live well
above the poverty line and the very considerable number

who live in comparative well-being have, on the other hand, occasioned much less comment. While in 1988 the top 1 percent of family groups had annual incomes that averaged $617,000 and controlled 13.5 percent of all income before taxes, the top 20 percent lived in conditions of some comfort with $50,000 a year and above. To them accrued 51.8 percent of all income before taxes.[1]

This latter income, or much of it, is, in turn, made relatively secure by a variety of public and private reinforcements — private pension funds, Social Security, publicly and privately sponsored and supported medical care, farm income supports and, very expensively, guarantees against loss because of the failure of financial institutions, banks and the now greatly celebrated savings and loan associations.

The substantial role of the government in subsidizing this well-being deserves more than passing notice. Where the impoverished are concerned — a point to which I will return — government support and subsidy are seriously suspect as to need and effectiveness of administration and because of their adverse effect on morals and working morale. This, however, is not true of government support to comparative well-being. By Social Security pensions or their prospect no one is thought damaged, nor, as a depositor, by being rescued from a failed bank. The com-

---

1. These figures were, in fact, only very modestly reduced by taxes. The posttax share of the top 1 percent was 12.8 percent; that of those with $50,000 was 49.8 percent. See the *Greenbook* of the Committee on Ways and Means of the United States House of Representatives, pp. 1308, 1309.

paratively affluent can withstand the adverse moral effect
of being subsidized and supported by the government; not
so the poor.

In past times, the economically and socially fortunate
were, as we know, a small minority — characteristically
a dominant and ruling handful. They are now a majority,
though, as has already been observed, a majority not of
all citizens but of those who actually vote. A convenient
reference is needed for those so situated and who so respond at the polls. They will be called the Contented
Majority, the Contented Electoral Majority or, more spa-
ciously, the Culture of Contentment. There will be adequate reiteration that this does not mean they are a
majority of all those eligible to vote. They rule under the
rich cloak of democracy, a democracy in which the less
fortunate do not participate. Nor does it mean — a most
important point — that they are silent in their contentment. They can be, as when this book goes to press, very
angry and very articulate about what seems to invade
their state of self-satisfaction.

While income broadly defines the contented majority, no
one should suppose that that majority is occupationally
or socially homogeneous. It includes the people who man-
age or otherwise staff the middle and upper reaches of the
great financial and industrial firms, independent business-
men and -women and those in lesser employments whose
compensation is more or less guaranteed. Also the large
population — lawyers, doctors, engineers, scientists, ac-

countants and many others, not excluding journalists and professors — who make up the modern professional class. Included also are a certain, if diminishing, number who once were called proletarians — those with diverse skills whose wages are now, with some frequency, supplemented by those of a diligent wife. They, like others in families with dual paychecks, find life reasonably secure.

Further, although they were once a strongly discontented community, there are the farmers, who, when buttressed by government price supports, are now amply rewarded.[2] Here too there is a dominant, if not universal, mood of satisfaction. Finally, there is the rapidly increasing number of the aged who live on pensions or other retirement allowance and for whose remaining years of life there is adequate or, on occasion, ample financial provision.

None of this suggests an absence of continuing personal aspiration or a unanimity of political view. Doing well, many wish to do better. Having enough, many wish for more. Being comfortable, many raise vigorous objection to that which invades comfort. What is important is that there is no self-doubt in their present situation. The future

2. "The average 1988 income of farm operator households was $33,535, compared with $34,017 for all U.S. households. However, 5 percent of farm operator households had incomes above $100,000, compared to 3.2 percent of all U.S. households." *Agricultural Income and Finance: Situation and Outlook Report* (Washington, D.C.: U.S. Department of Agriculture Economic Research Service, May 1990), p. 26.

for the contented majority is thought effectively within their personal command. Their anger is evident — and, indeed, can be strongly evident — only when there is a threat or possible threat to present well-being and future prospect — when government and the seemingly less deserving intrude or threaten to intrude their needs or demands. This is especially so if such action suggests higher taxes.

As to political attitude, there is a minority, not small in number, who do look beyond personal contentment to a concern for those who do not share in the comparative well-being. Or they see the more distant dangers that will result from a short-run preoccupation with individual comfort. Idealism and foresight are not dead; on the contrary, their expression is the most reputable form of social discourse. While self-interest, as we shall see, does frequently operate under a formal cover of social concern, much social concern is genuinely and generously motivated.

Nonetheless, self-regard is, and predictably, the dominant, indeed the controlling, mood of the contented majority. This becomes wholly evident when public action on behalf of those outside this electoral majority is the issue. If it is to be effective, such action is invariably at public cost. Accordingly, it is regularly resisted as a matter of high, if sometimes rather visibly contrived, principle. Of this, more later.

*

In the recent past much has been held wrong with the performance of the United States government as regards both domestic and foreign policy. This has been widely attributed to the inadequacy, incompetence or generally perverse performance of individual politicians and political leaders. Mr. Reagan and his now accepted intellectual and administrative detachment, and Mr. Bush, his love of travel and his belief in oratory as the prime instrument of domestic action, have been often cited. Similarly criticized have been leaders and members of the Congress, and, if less stridently, governors and other politicians throughout the Republic.

This criticism, or much of it, is mistaken or, at best, politically superficial. The government of the United States in recent years has been a valid reflection of the economic and social preferences of the majority of those voting — the electoral majority. In defense of Ronald Reagan and George Bush as Presidents, it must be said and emphasized that both were, or are, faithful representatives of the constituency that elected them. We attribute to politicians what should be attributed to the community they serve.

The first and most general expression of the contented majority is its affirmation that those who compose it are receiving their just deserts. What the individual member aspires to have and enjoy is the product of his or her personal virtue, intelligence and effort. Good fortune being earned or the reward of merit, there is no equitable justification for any action that impairs it — that subtracts from what is enjoyed or might be enjoyed. The normal response to such action is indignation or, as suggested, anger at anything infringing on what is so clearly deserved.

There will, as noted, be individuals — on frequent occasion in the past, some who have inherited what they have — who will be less certain that they merit their comparative good fortune. And more numerous will be those scholars, journalists, professional dissidents and other voices who will express sympathy for the excluded and concern for the future, often from positions of relative personal comfort. The result will be political effort and agitation in conflict with the aims and preferences of the contented. The number so motivated is, to repeat, not small, but they are not a serious threat to the electoral majority. On the contrary, by their dissent they give a gracing aspect of democracy to the ruling position of the fortunate. They show in their articulate way that "democracy is working." Liberals in the United States, Labour politicians and spokesmen in Britain, are, indeed, vital in this regard. Their writing and rhetoric give hope to the excluded and, at a minimum, assure that they are not both excluded *and* ignored.

Highly convenient social and economic doctrine also emerges in defense of contentment, some of which is modern and some ancient. As will be seen, what once justified the favored position of the few — a handful of aristocrats or capitalists — has now become the favoring defense of the comfortable many.

The second, less conscious but extremely important characteristic of the contented majority, one already noted, is its attitude toward time. In the briefest word, short-run public inaction, even if held to be alarming as to consequence, is always preferred to protective long-run action. The reason is readily evident. The long run may not arrive; that is the frequent and comfortable belief. More decisively important, the cost of today's action falls or could fall on the favored community; taxes could be increased. The benefits in the longer run may well be for others to enjoy. In any case, the quiet theology of laissez faire holds that all will work out for the best in the end.

Here too there will be contrary voices. These will be heard, and often with respect, but not to the point of action. For the contented majority the logic of inaction is inescapable. For many years, for example, there has been grave concern in the northeastern United States and extending up to Canada over acid rain caused by sulphurous emissions from the power plants of the Midwest. The long-run effects will, it is known, be extremely adverse — on the environment, the recreational industries, the forest industry, maple sugar producers and on the general benignity of local life and scene. The cost of corrective measures to the electric power plants and their consumers will be immediate and specific, while the longer-term conservation reward will, in contrast, be diffuse, uncertain and debatable as to specific incidence. From this comes the policy avowed by the contented. It does not deny the problem, this not being possible; rather, it delays action. Notably, it proposes more research, which very often provides a comforting, intellectually reputable gloss over inaction. At the worst, it suggests impaneling a commission, the purpose of which would be to discuss and recommend action or perhaps postponement thereof. At the very worst, there is limited, perhaps symbolic, action, as in recent times. Other long-run environmental dangers — global warming and the dissipation of the ozone layer — invite a similar response.

Another example of the role of time is seen in attitudes toward what is called, rather formidably, the economic infrastructure of the United States — its highways, bridges, airports, mass transportation facilities and other public structures. These are now widely perceived as falling far below future need and even present standards of safety. Nonetheless, expenditure and new investment in this area are powerfully and effectively resisted. Again the very plausible reason: present cost and taxation are specific; future advantage is dispersed. Later and different individuals will benefit; why pay for persons unknown? So again the readily understandable insistence on inaction and the resulting freedom from present cost. Contentment is here revealed to be of growing social influence, more decisive than in the past. The interstate highway system, the parkways, the airports, even perhaps the hospitals and schools of an earlier and financially far more astringent time but one when the favored voters were far fewer, could not be built today.

In the 1980s the preference for short-run advantage was dramatically evident, as will later be noted, in the continued deficits in the budget of the United States and in the related and resulting deficits in the international trade accounts. Here the potential cost to the favored voting community, the contented electoral majority, was highly specific. To reduce the deficit meant more taxation or a reduction in expenditures, including those important to the comfortable. The distant benefits seemed, predictably, diffuse and uncertain as to impact. Again no one can doubt that Presidents Reagan and Bush were or are in highly sympathetic response to their constituency on this matter. While criticism of their action or inaction has been inevitable, their instinct as to what their politically decisive supporters wanted has been impeccable.

A third commitment of the comfortably situated is to a highly selective view of the role of the state — of government. Broadly and superficially speaking, the state is seen as a burden; no political avowal of modern times has been so often reiterated and so warmly applauded as the need "to get government off the backs of the people." The albatross was not hung more oppressively by his shipmates around the neck of the Mariner. The need to lighten or remove this burden and therewith, agreeably, the supporting taxes is an article of high faith for the comfortable or contented majority.

But while government in general has been viewed as a burden, there have been, as will be seen, significant and costly exceptions from this broad condemnation. Excluded from criticism, needless to say, have been Social Security, medical care at higher income levels, farm income supports and financial guarantees to depositors in ill-fated banks and savings and loan enterprises. These are strong supports to the comfort and security of the contented majority. No one would dream of attacking them, even marginally, in any electoral contest.

Specifically favored also have been military expenditures, their scale and fiscally oppressive effect notwithstanding. This has been for three reasons. These expenditures, as they are reflected in the economy in wages, salaries, profits and assorted subsidies to research and other institutions, serve to sustain or enhance the income of a considerable segment of the contented electoral majority. Weapons expenditure, unlike, for example, spending for the urban poor, rewards a very comfortable constituency.

More important, perhaps, military expenditures, as also those for the associated operations of the CIA and to a diminishing extent the Department of State, have been seen in the past as vital protection against the gravest perceived threat to continued comfort and contentment.

That threat was from Communism, with its clear and overt, even if remote, endangerment of the economic life and rewards of the comfortable. This fear, in turn, extending on occasion to clinical paranoia, assured support to the military establishment. And American liberals, no less than conservatives, felt obliged, given their personal commitment to liberty and human rights, to show by their support of defense spending that they were not "soft on Communism."

The natural focus of concern was the Soviet Union and its once seemingly stalwart satellites in Eastern Europe. Fear of the not inconsiderable competence of the Soviets in military technology and production provided the main pillar of support for American military spending. However, the alarm was geographically comprehensive. It supported expenditure and military action against such improbable threats as those from Angola, Afghanistan, Ethiopia, Grenada, El Salvador, Nicaragua, Laos, Cambodia and, massively, tragically and at great cost, from Vietnam. From being considered a source of fear and concern, only Communist China was, from the early 1970s on, exempt. Turning against the Soviet Union and forgiven for its earlier role in Korea and Vietnam, it became an honorary bastion of democracy and free enterprise, which, later repressive actions notwithstanding, it rather substantially remains.

The final reason that military expenditures have continued to be favored is the self-perpetuating power of the military and weapons establishment itself — its control of the weaponry it is to produce, the missions for which it is to be prepared, in substantial measure the funds that it receives and dispenses.

Until World War II, the fortunately situated in the United States, the Republican Party in particular, resisted military expenditures, as they then resisted all government spending. In the years since, the presumed worldwide Communist menace, as frequently it was designated, brought a major reversal: those with a comfortable concern for their own economic position became the most powerful advocates of the most prodigal of military outlays. With the collapse of Communism, an interesting question arises as to what the attitude of the contented will now be. That the military establishment, public and private, will continue on its own authority to claim a large share of its past financial support is not, however, seriously in doubt.

Such are the exceptions that the contented majority makes to its general condemnation of government as a burden. Social expenditure favorable to the fortunate, financial rescue, military spending and, of course, interest payments — these constitute in the aggregate by far the largest part of the federal budget and that which in recent times has shown by far the greatest increase. What remains — expenditures for welfare, low-cost housing, health care for those otherwise unprotected, public edu-

cation and the diverse needs of the great urban slums —
is what is now viewed as the burden of government. It is
uniquely that which serves the interests of those outside
the contented electoral majority; it is, and inescapably,
what serves the poor. Here again Mr. Reagan and now Mr.
Bush showed or now show a keen sense of their constituency. So also they do with regard to one further tendency
of the contented majority.

The final characteristic here to be cited and stressed is
the tolerance shown by the contented of great differences
in income. These differences have already been noted, as
has the fact that the disparity is not a matter that occasions serious dispute. A general and quite plausible convention is here observed: the price of prevention of any
aggression against one's own income is tolerance of the
greater amount for others. Indignation at, and advocacy
of, redistribution of income from the very rich, inevitably
by taxes, opens the door for consideration of higher taxes
for the comfortable but less endowed. This is especially
a threat given the position and possible claims of the least
favored part of the population. Any outcry from the fortunate half could only focus attention on the far inferior
position of the lower half. The plush advantage of the
very rich is the price the contented electoral majority pays
for being able to retain what is less but what is still very
good. And, it is averred, there could be solid social advantage in this tolerance of the very fortunate: "To help

the poor and middle classes, one must cut the taxes on the rich."[3]

Ronald Reagan's single most celebrated economic action, the acceptance of the related budget deficit possibly apart, was his tax relief for the very affluent. Marginal rates on the very rich were reduced from a partly nominal 70 percent to 50 percent in 1981; then with tax reform the rate on the richest fell to 28 percent in 1986, although this was partly offset by other tax changes. The result was a generous increase in the after-tax income in the higher income brackets. That part of Mr. Reagan's motivation was his memory of the presumptively painful tax demands on his Hollywood pay seems not in doubt. He was also influenced by the economic ideas that had been adapted to serve tax reduction on the rich — broadly, the doctrine that if the horse is fed amply with oats, some will pass through to the road for the sparrows. But once again there was also the sense of what served his larger constituency, as well as that of the concurring Congress. This constituency accepted the favor to the very rich in return for protection for itself.

In summary, we see that much that has been attributed in these past years to ideology, idiosyncrasy or error of political leadership has deep roots in the American polity.

---

3. George Gilder, *Wealth and Poverty* (New York: Basic Books, 1981), p. 188. He is quoted by Kevin Phillips in *The Politics of Rich and Poor: Wealth and the American Electorate in the Reagan Aftermath* (New York: Random House, 1990), p. 62.

It has been said, and often, in praise of Ronald Reagan as President that he gave the American people a good feeling about themselves. This acclaim is fully justified as regards the people who voted for him, and even perhaps as regards that not inconsiderable number who, voting otherwise, found themselves in silent approval of the very tangible personal effect of his tax policies.

In past times in the United States, under government by either of the major parties, many experienced a certain sense of unease, of troubled conscience and associated discomfort when contemplating those who did not share the good fortune of the fortunate. No such feeling emanated from Ronald Reagan; Americans were being rewarded as they so richly deserved. If some did not participate, it was because of their inability or by their choice. As it was once the privilege of Frenchmen, both the rich and the poor, to sleep under bridges, so any American had the undoubted right to sleep on street grates. This might not be the reality, but it was the presidentially ordained script. And this script was tested by Ronald Reagan, out of his long and notable theatrical training, not for its reality, not for its truth, but, as if it were a motion picture or a television commercial, for its appeal. That appeal was widespread; it allowed Americans to escape their consciences and their social concerns and thus to feel a glow of self-approval.

Not all, of course, could so feel, nor, necessarily, could a majority of all citizens of voting age. And there was a further and socially rather bitter circumstance, one that has been conveniently neglected: the comfort and economic well-being of the contented majority was being supported and enhanced by the presence in the modern economy of a large, highly useful, even essential class that does not share in the agreeable existence of the favored community. To the nature and services of this class, here denoted the Functional Underclass, I now turn.

3

The Functional Underclass

THERE HAS BEEN REFERENCE in the previous chapter to class; on no matter is American social thought in its accepted and popular manifestation more insistent than on social class or, more specifically, the absence thereof in the United States. We have a classless society; to this we point with considerable pride. The social mythology of the Republic is built on the concept of classlessness — the belief, as President George Bush once put it, that class is "for European democracies or something else — it isn't for the United States of America. We are not going to be divided by class."[1]

Yet truth, if sufficiently obvious and inescapable, does obtrude. Presidential oratory, however well-intended and even eloquent, does not serve entirely to suppress it. Determinedly and irrevocably into the American language has come the modern reference to "the underclass." There

---

1. Quoted in Benjamin DeMott, *The Imperial Middle: Why Americans Can't Think Straight About Class* (New York: Morrow, 1990), pp. 9–10.

are individuals and families that, it is conceded, do not share the comfortable well-being of the prototypical American. These people, this class, are concentrated, as I have already indicated, in the centers of the great cities or, less visibly, on deprived farms, as rural migrant labor or in erstwhile mining communities. Or they are the more diffused poor of the Old South and of the region of the Rio Grande in Texas. The greater part of the underclass consists of members of minority groups, blacks or people of Hispanic origin. While the most common reference is to the underclass of the great cities, this is at least partly because its presence there is the most inescapably apparent.

So much is accepted. What is not accepted, and indeed is little mentioned, is that the underclass is integrally a part of a larger economic process and, more importantly, that it serves the living standard and the comfort of the more favored community. Economic progress would be far more uncertain and certainly far less rapid without it. The economically fortunate, not excluding those who speak with greatest regret of the existence of this class, are heavily dependent on its presence.

The underclass is deeply functional; all industrial countries have one in greater or lesser measure and in one form or another. As some of its members escape from deprivation and its associated compulsions, a resupply becomes essential. But on few matters, it must be added, is even the most sophisticated economic and social comment more reticent. The picture of an economic and political system in which social exclusion, however unforgiving, is somehow a remediable affliction is all but required. Here, in highly compelling fashion, the social convenience of the contented replaces the clearly visible reality.

Appreciation of this reality begins with the popular, indeed obligatory, definition of work. Work, in the conventional view, is pleasant and rewarding; it is something in which all favored by occupation rejoice to a varying degree. A normal person is proud of his or her work.

In practical fact, much work is repetitive, tedious, painfully fatiguing, mentally boring or socially demeaning. This is true of diverse consumer and household services and the harvesting of farm crops, and is equally true in those industries that deploy workers on assembly lines, where labor cost is a major factor in the price of what is finally produced. Only, or in any case primarily, when this nexus between labor cost and price is broken or partly disassociated, invariably at higher income levels, does work become pleasant and, in fact, enjoyed. It is a basic but rarely articulated feature of the modern economic system that the highest pay is given for the work that is most prestigious and most agreeable. This is at the opposite extreme from those occupations that are inherently invidious, those that place the individual directly under the command of another, as in the case of the doorman or the household servant, and those involving a vast range of tasks — street cleaning, garbage collection, janitorial services, elevator operation — that have an obtrusive connotation of social inferiority.

There is no greater modern illusion, even fraud, than the use of the single term *work* to cover what for some is, as noted, dreary, painful or socially demeaning and what for others is enjoyable, socially reputable and economically rewarding. Those who spend pleasant, well-compensated days say with emphasis that they have been "hard at work," thereby suppressing the notion that they are a favored class. They are, of course, allowed to say that they enjoy their work, but it is presumed that such enjoyment is shared by any *good* worker. In a brief moment of truth, we speak, when sentencing criminals, of years at "hard labor." Otherwise we place a common gloss over what is agreeable and what, to a greater or lesser extent, is endured or suffered.

From the foregoing comes one of the basic facts of modern economic society: the poor in our economy are needed to do the work that the more fortunate do not do and would find manifestly distasteful, even distressing. And a continuing supply and resupply of such workers is always needed. That is because later generations do not wish to follow their parents into physically demanding, socially unacceptable or otherwise disagreeable occupations; they escape or seek to escape the heavy lifting to a more comfortable and rewarding life. This we fully understand and greatly approve; it is what education is generally meant to accomplish. But from this comes the need for the resupply or, less agreeably, for keeping some part of the underclass in continued and deferential subjection.

To see these matters in the clearest light, one must first look at their resolution in Western Europe.

In the last forty years in Germany, France and Switzerland, and in lesser measure in Austria and Scandinavia, the provision of outside workers for the tasks for which indigenous laborers are no longer available has been both accepted and highly organized. The factories of the erstwhile German Federal Republic are manned, and a broad range of other work is performed, by Turks and Yugoslavs. Those in France are similarly supplied by what amounts to a new invasion of the Moors — the vast influx from the former North African colonies. Switzerland has long relied on Italian and Spanish workers. The industrial north of Italy, in turn, has depended heavily on a reserve army of the unemployed from the south — the more backward Mezzogiorno — and now increasingly from North Africa. The British economy has been sustained in no small part by migrants from the former dominions — India, Pakistan, Bangladesh and the West Indies.

The employment of these workers goes beyond manufacturing establishments and factory assembly lines to a wide range of jobs. Restaurants, household and other personal services and less elegant public employments are all their conceded domain. In the large and generally excellent Swiss hospitals, decline and death would, it is said, be probable, if not inevitable, in the absence of the menial foreign staff. Swiss highways would not be repaired without them, or snow or city garbage removed. This is work that the older Swiss work force does not do. Nor, to repeat, do native workers man the assembly lines or undertake the nonprestigious tasks in Germany, France or elsewhere in Western Europe in any nearly sufficient way.

There are marked further advantages in this arrangement — in the availability of this admitted underclass. If it becomes unneeded, it can be sent home or, as more often, denied entry. This has been accomplished in Switzerland with such precision in the past that involuntary unemployment has been often in the low hundreds. Most important of all, these workers, coming as they do from countries and occupations (mostly poor and tedious peasant agriculture) with much lower incomes, are impressed by their new comparative well-being. They are not, accordingly, as assertive as to wage and other claims as would be local workers, and their assertiveness is further tempered by the fact that they are not, with some progressive exceptions, voting and participating citizens. Many, once a certain financial competence is acquired, plan to return home. And some may have entered the country illegally, which usefully enforces their silence.

Not much has been made of this migration, some ethnic

tension apart, and even less of the fact that in the years since World War II it has been essential for Western European economic life. That is because the offspring of the traditional older working class have gone on to the more pleasant and remunerative employments, the employments that are also called work. Still less has been made of a functionally similar underclass in the United States. Here too it has one of the uncelebrated but indispensable roles in modern capitalism. Both its character and also its uses are, however, rather more ambiguous and diverse than those of the foreign workers in Europe, those who are often called guest workers to emphasize their seemingly temporary role.

In the latter years of the last century and until World War I, American mass-employment industry and the less agreeable urban occupations drew their work force extensively from Eastern Europe as well as from the labor surplus of American farms. As this supply diminished, poor whites from the Appalachian plateau and, in greatly increasing numbers, blacks from the South moved to take their place. The assembly plants and body shops of Detroit were once staffed by workers from the adjacent farms and small towns of Michigan and Ontario, as well as by immigrants from Poland and elsewhere in Europe. As that generation went on to personally more attractive or socially more distinguished occupations, the assembly lines there reached out to more distant refugees from poor farming and mining areas and to the erstwhile sharecroppers and other deprived rural workers of the Deep South. With the latter recruitment Detroit became a city of largely black population; the automobile industry would not have survived had it had to rely on the sons and daughters of its original workers. Nor would many other public and private services have been available in tolerable form.

In more recent times, migration from Mexico, Latin America and the West Indies has become a general source of such labor. For many years now, legal provision has been made for the importation of workers for the harvesting of fruit and vegetables, there being very specific acknowledgment that this is something native-born Americans cannot be persuaded in the necessary numbers to do. There is here, somewhat exceptionally, a clear legal perception of the role of the underclass.

In the immigration legislation of 1990, there was at last some official recognition of the more general and continuing need for immigrant labor. Although much of the discussion of this measure turned on the opening of the door to needed skilled workers (and compassionately to relatives of earlier migrants), the larger purpose was not in doubt. There would be a new and necessary recruitment of men and women to do the tasks of the underclass. Avoided only was mention of such seemingly brutal truth. It is not thought appropriate to say that the modern economy — the market system — requires such an underclass, and certainly not that it must reach out to other countries to sustain and refresh it.

*

37

It is important to note and emphasize that the contribution of the underclass is not confined to disagreeable industrial and agricultural employment. In the modern urban community, as noted, there is a vast range of tedious or socially demeaning jobs that require unskilled, willing and adequately inexpensive labor. To this need the underclass responds, and it makes urban life at the comfortable levels of well-being not only pleasant but possible. There is, however, the darker side.

In the inner cities of the United States, as less dramatically in Europe — Brixton and Notting Hill Gate in London, areas in France where North African migrants are heavily concentrated — there is a continuing threat of underclass social disorder, crime and conflict. Drug dealing, indiscriminate gunfire, other crime and family disorientation and disintegration are now all aspects of everyday existence.

In substantial part, this is because a less vigorously expanding economy and the movement of industry to economically more favored locations have denied to the underclass those relatively stable and orderly industrial employments once available in the large cities. But also, and more importantly, the normal upward movement that was for long the solvent for discontent has been arrested. The underclass has become a semipermanent rather than a generational phenomenon. There has been surprisingly little comment as to why minority communities in New York, Chicago, Los Angeles and elsewhere, once poor but benign and culturally engaging, are now centers of terror and despair. The reason is that what was a favoring upward step in economic life has now become a hopeless enthrallment.

Yet, considering the sordid life to which the modern underclass is committed, and especially when their life is compared with that of the contented majority, it is an occasion for wonder that the discontent and its more violent and aggressive manifestations are not greater than they are. One reason, evident in Europe and also important in the United States, is that for some of the underclass life in the cities, although insecure, ill-rewarded and otherwise primitive, still remains, if tenuously, better than that from which they escaped. The great black migration to the North after World War II was from a rural existence, classically that of the sharecropper, with rudimentary shelter and clothing; no health care; hard farm labor; exploitative living costs; little in the way of schooling; no voting rights; forthright, accepted and enforced racial discrimination; and, withal, extreme invisibility. Urban life, however unsatisfactory, was an improvement. So also for those moving from Puerto Rico and in the recent past from Latin America. For many the comparison is not with those who are more fortunate but with their own past position. This latter comparison and its continuing memory in the culture unquestionably has had the same tranquilizing effect on the American underclass as it has on that in Europe. It is one unnoted reason, along with ineligibility because of recent arrival or illegal presence, that underclass voter turnout in elections is relatively low.

While the urban areas inhabited by the underclass have seen outbreaks of violence in the past, notably the widespread riots in the second half of the 1960s, the more surprising thing, nonetheless, is their relative tranquillity. This, however, it will be evident from the foregoing, is something on which no one should count in the future. It has existed in the past because, as noted, the underclass has been in the process of transition — that from a lesser life, and with the prospect of generational escape. As this process comes to an end — as membership in the underclass becomes stable and enduring — greater resentment and social unrest should be expected. A blockage in the movement upward and out of the underclass will not be accepted. However, although it will not be accepted, it will not in the ordinary course of events be anticipated.

It is not in the nature of the politics of contentment to expect or plan countering action for misfortune, even disaster, that, however predictable and predicted, is in the yet undisclosed future. Such planning, invoking as it always does public action — provision of good educational opportunity, good public housing and health care, competent attention to drug addiction, family counseling, adequate welfare payments — is systemically resisted by the contented electoral majority. In what is the accepted and, indeed, only acceptable view, the underclass is deemed the source of its own succor and well-being; in the extreme view, it requires the spur of its own poverty, and it will be damaged by any social assistance and support. None of this is, of course, quite believed; it serves, nonetheless, to justify the comfortable position and policy.

4

Taxation and
the Public Services

THE PERVERSE EFFECT

TAXATION, it has been observed, plays a compelling role in the culture of contentment. Notable is the already mentioned constraint that keeps the only modestly fortunate from urging higher taxes on the top fifth of the population, although the income of the latter is now more than that of the other four-fifths. There is at work here a companionate acceptance of inequality in order to protect against the common enemy, which is higher taxes on all.

Taxation and attitudes thereto, as will later be stressed, have also come to have a decisive effect on the overall management of the economy. Once, in the days of triumph of John Maynard Keynes in the 1930s and after, it was widely agreed that when inflation threatened, public expenditures should, to the extent possible, be curtailed and taxes should be increased in order to reduce the flow of purchasing power — in economic parlance, the aggregate demand — and thus lessen the upward pressure on markets and prices. Symmetrically, taxes should be reduced when recession threatened, when there was need to augment the flow of consumer demand. Now such a line of policy, though surviving in the textbooks, has, in any practical sense, been relegated to the museums wherein are kept the numerous past idiosyncrasies of economic thought. To raise taxes in the face of inflation is to risk that later, when they are unneeded, they may not be reduced. And, with whatever theoretical support, it would still be an increase in taxation.

Now, in the age of contentment, what economists call macroeconomic policy has come to center not on tax policy but on monetary policy — the mediating actions of the central bank, in the United States the Federal Reserve System. Higher interest rates, it is hoped, will curb inflation; in any case, they will not threaten men and women of good fortune. Those with money to lend, the economically well endowed rentier class, will thus be rewarded. A recession in modern times bring reluctant decrease in interest rates. Perhaps, at most, there will be a reduction in taxes always with the chance that that reduction will be permanent.

In everyday economic treatment, monetary and fiscal policy are both held to be socially and politically neutral; at issue only is the wisdom of the choice between them in the particular circumstance and time. There could be no greater error. As is not wholly exceptional in economics, there is here a serious disguise of politically inconvenient reality. The modern reliance on monetary policy and the rejection of tax and expenditure policy emerge from the entirely plausible and powerfully adverse attitude toward taxation in the community of contentment. To the role of monetary policy in this context I will return.

There is an even more urgent barrier to taxation in the political economy of contentment. That is the marked asymmetry between who pays and who receives. For a considerable, though by no means the entire, range of public services, the supporting taxes fall on the contented; the benefits accrue to others. In particular, the fortunate in the polity find themselves paying through their taxes the public cost of the functional underclass, and this, in the most predictable of economic responses, they resist. There follows a highly understandable resistance to all taxation.

Thus, in the United States, as in the other industrial lands, the poorest people must rely on the government for publicly subsidized shelter. In no economically advanced country — a sadly neglected matter — does the market system build houses the poor can afford. There is also reliance on the government in the United States for food — for food stamps and the welfare and child support that prevent starvation. Housing and food the comfortably situated provide for themselves as a matter of course.

And, in less marked manner, the same is true of education. Whereas the poor have no alternative to the public schools, the more fortunate pay separately, in effect, for their own. These are either the better-financed public schools of the more affluent suburbs or private schools. In the latter case, the fortunate have to pay twice, and one of their more plausible reactions is the recurrent suggestion that they should be remitted the equivalent of the taxes they pay for public education in a voucher usable for private schools of their choice. Thus they would escape the burden of the double educational cost. By convention, however, this is not put so rudely; freedom of choice, liberty, the wise privatization of public activity — these are the most frequently heard justifications.

The perverse relationship between taxes and public services extends on. The poor need public parks and recreational facilities; in the suburbs these become of diminished importance, and the very affluent have and enjoy private clubs, golf courses and tennis courts. The poor need public libraries; the more fortunate can buy books or they have libraries of their own. Many of the poor live in the inner cities, where police presence is necessary every day; in the suburbs such protection is of less urgency and, in any case, is specific in its services to those comfortably there resident. For those at yet higher levels of income, there are private security guards, their number now exceeding the number of publicly employed policemen in the United States. Less ostentatiously there are doormen and alarm systems to alert and protect the occupants of the better urban apartment buildings.[1] Public hospitals and public health services at public cost are essential for those of lesser income; the comfortable have access to private hospitals and health insurance. As with the schools, they must, in the end, pay for both public and their own private health care.

From the foregoing comes the broad attitude toward taxes in our time and, in substantial measure, toward government in general. The fortunate pay, the less fortunate receive. The fortunate have political voice, the less fortunate do not. It would be an exercise in improbably charitable attitude were the fortunate to respond warmly to expenditures that are for the benefit of others. So government with all its costs is pictured as a functionless burden, which for the fortunate, to a considerable extent, it is. Accordingly, it and the sustaining taxes must be kept to a minimum; otherwise, the liberty of the individual will be impaired.

And politicians faithfully respond. To run for office promising better services for those most in need at even

1. Robert B. Reich, detailing the above matters with his accustomed diligence, has also come upon special public-service arrangements in New York for cleaning the streets in specific urban neighborhoods, thus relieving residents of the effects of declining sanitation in the city as a whole. See "Secession of the Successful," *The New York Times Magazine*, January 20, 1991. Adapted from *The Work of Nations: Preparing Ourselves for 21st-Century Capitalism* (New York: Knopf, 1991).

higher cost is seen by many, if not quite all, as an exercise in political self-destruction.

In ordinary discourse there is little or no mention of the disparity of interest between those who receive more but pay less and those who need less but pay more. This could be an unwelcome source of moral disquiet. Instead, as has already been noted, government is held to be inefficient, incompetent, in motivated assault on private well-being and, above all, a burden. The practical manifestation of these deficiencies is taxation; accordingly, it must be urgently, even righteously, resisted. With this resistance, needless to say, goes strong, often indignant resistance to increased public services, for, without being of benefit to the electoral majority, they might seem to justify increased taxes.

There is here in practical politics a highly visible association between taxation and public expenditures. Expenditures, with exceptions later to be noted and stressed, are under the broad suspicion of government activity and, inevitably, threaten increased taxation. And the reverse effect is also true: resistance to higher taxation is seen as a way of limiting public functions and services. Any increase in tax revenues, it is held, will go not for the necessary purposes of the state; rather, it will be appropriated by those whose commitment is to expenditure per se. It will be appropriated by the dedicated "big spenders."

Thus, the Reagan administration made opposition to

tax increases and, in fact, a substantial reduction in income taxes a central instrument of policy. And President Bush was no less specific: his pre-election promise not to raise taxes was, by some margin, the best publicized of his policy commitments. Both men saw a restriction on taxes as a design for restraining government activity as a whole, the favored exceptions apart. Both, it is clear, were responding not, as some thought, to a personal political view; they were correctly interpreting the highly evident preference of the contented electoral majority. President Reagan was warmly supported by this constituency; when President Bush seemed even marginally to defect from its interests by accepting a small tax increase in 1990, he was severely criticized.

It must be stressed again that the reaction of the contented majority to the costs and purposes of government has a selective aspect. There are some public services and functions that have their approval. Defense is the clearest case, serving in the past as the obvious antidote to their deep, even paranoiac fear of Communism. Now, with the collapse of that presumed enemy, the industries involved still draw on their own indigenous political power.

Similarly, support to failing financial institutions — the great savings and loan rescue and later that of the commercial banks — is a fully defended function of the government, however evident the financial extravagance and extensive and visible larceny that made it necessary. Were the appropriations for these rescue operations applied instead to government expenditures for welfare, they would be deemed burdensome and otherwise wholly intolerable.

To summarize: public services and taxation have a disparate impact on the contented electoral majority on the one hand and on the less affluent underclass on the other, and it is this difference that has clearly and plausibly produced the tax and fiscal policies of these last years. One part of the community pays the taxes and votes; another receives the benefits and does not vote. In pursuit of the self-interest of those with vote and voice, it has been held that taxes should be reduced and not thereafter increased in any visible way; welfare services should, to the extent possible, be curtailed. There should not, however, be any reduction in favored expenditures, especially those for defense and financial-rescue operations. The result of lowered taxes without suitably lowered expenditures has been a large and continuing budget deficit. That deficit, financed by borrowing, has had longer-run effects, including, obviously, the necessary expenditures for interest, as also the adverse effect of the necessarily high interest rates on industrial productivity. But to longer-run consequences the culture of contentment does not, as we have seen, respond.

The Reagan and Bush administrations have not escaped criticism for the policies aforementioned — the cutting of welfare and similar expenditures, the cutting of taxes with its special benefit to the very rich, the resistance to tax increases, and the deficit. All of these have been held to be deficient in compassion, damaging on broad economic policy grounds and even politically unwise.[2] What has not been stressed or even much mentioned is their careful reflection of the controlling political context. Those pursuing these policies have been reacting faithfully to the will of their constituency, the contented electoral majority. They have, indeed, been faithful to democratic principle, always allowing for the fact that this is a democracy in which, broadly speaking, the fortunate have the commanding voice and vote.

A final point must be emphasized: the matters here discussed are not a subject for either surprise or indignation. There is nothing unusual about the pursuit of self-interest; it is widely and, in much of life, quite justly celebrated. The purpose here, as ever, is to see it clearly in all its manifestations and social effects.

2. For example, in the interesting and also, to many, distressing work of Kevin Phillips, *The Politics of Rich and Poor: Wealth and the American Electorate in the Reagan Aftermath* (New York: Random House, 1990).

5

The License for Financial Devastation

In this world the follies of the rich
pass for wise sayings.

CENTRAL TO THE ECONOMICS of contentment is
the general commitment to laissez faire. This is
not a formally avowed principle — or, in any
case, it is not often so affirmed. Rather, it is an attitude,
the belief that it is in the nature of things, and especially
of economic life, that all works out for the best in the
end. Nothing that happens in the short run is in conflict
with longer-run well-being. The intervention of the state,
with its controlling or sustaining hand, is not necessary,
and except as a bank or a corporation needs to be rescued
or the common defense furthered, it is never benign. One
does not countenance interference with what is pro-
grammed to work or, to repeat, with what will work in
the longer run whatever the adverse short-run experience
or whatever the warning or prediction as to the future.

So much is in the area of largely unexpressed faith. The

specific instrument for ensuring benignity, specifically cited and avowed, is the market. Here public authority is sharply forbidden to interfere, for to do so is to impair or frustrate the operation of the very mechanism that ensures socially rewarding performance. With the market, attitude becomes formal controlling doctrine.

That the market does not produce socially optimal results has, in fact, been long recognized by economists. There is monopoly, and there are numerous lesser imperfections of competition. This is accepted, as also, in large measure, the visibly unequal distribution of power between employer and employed and an intrinsically and even egregiously unequal distribution of income. A very large part of all modern economic expression, extending on to political debate and action, has concerned these less than socially equitable aspects of the market. Public programs, many of them broadly identified with the welfare state — old-age pensions, unemployment compensation, public health care, antitrust legislation, housing for the poor, environmental and consumer protection, progressive income taxation and support to trade unions — have clearly mitigated the inequities and cruelties of the system and, in doing so, have gone far to ensure the survival of capitalism. But invariably, as we have seen, such action has been most resisted by those whose economic position has been placed most at risk by the political reaction or community violence resulting from the aforementioned injustices of the market. This, the short-run response, is normal.

So much is accepted — or, in any case, is recognized as the substance of present-day political debate. Both those who support and those who oppose welfare measures can thus claim to be defenders of the system. What is not accepted and is, indeed, unrecognized is the powerful tendency of the economic system to turn damagingly not on consumers, workers or the public at large, but ruthlessly inward on itself. Under the broad and benign cover of laissez faire and the specific license of the market, there are forces that ravage and even destroy the very institutions that compose the system, specifically the business firms whose buying, selling and financial operations make the market. This is a striking development of modern capitalism; the particular devastation is of the great management-controlled corporation. Such destruction has become especially severe in the years of contentment. That it is an intrinsic feature of the uncontrolled market system is, as I've said, still largely unrecognized. Though much noted in economic writing and reporting, it has been seen primarily as an episodic development and not as something that is the product of inner causation.

The self-destructive tendency of modern capitalism begins with the large corporation. It has long been accepted that here effective power passes with a firm inevitability from the owners or stockholders to the management. The stockholders are numerous and dispersed; individual votes count for little or, more often, for nothing. The knowledge requisite for stockholder intervention in the diverse and complex affairs of the enterprise, some larger holdings apart, is lacking; in the clearest statement of where the authority lies, it is the management that selects the members of the board of directors, which then, ostensibly, represents the stockholders. As early as the 1930s and 1940s, distinguished scholars, among them a committed conservative, described the euthanasia of stockholder power and the dominance of managerial power.[1]

Out of the foregoing has come the basic anomaly of large corporate enterprise in the market system. It is assumed in all established economic doctrine that the business firm seeks to maximize its profits. For that it exists; any other purpose would reject the basic tendency of human nature. In so doing and, in the words of Adam Smith, through no intention of its own, it serves the public interest. The presumption, celebrated as theologically immutable doctrine, is that profit is maximized for the owners, the stockholders, the capitalists.

But here is the anomaly: it is the management that has the power, and the management, that power notwithstanding, is presumed to surrender its own interest to the interest of the stockholders, who are singularly without power. Thus worked into the justifying theory of the cor-

1. The decisive work was that of Adolf A. Berle, Jr., and Gardiner C. Means, *The Modern Corporation and Private Property* (New York: Commerce Clearing House, 1932). James Burnham, the undeviating conservative, affirmed the dominant role of management in *The Managerial Revolution: What Is Happening in the World* (New York: John Day, 1941).

poration is both the assumption of unrelenting profit maximization and a largely selfless surrender of the resulting gains by those responsible for such maximization. In fact, the assumption of self-interest is valid. As managers have escaped the control of stockholders, they have come increasingly to maximize their own return. The revenue enhancement by management has been in the form of salaries and stock options; retirement benefits; exceptionally diverse and expensive perquisites, with some special emphasis on aircraft; more mundane expense accounts; golden parachutes as protection if there is loss of power; and other financial rewards.[2] In 1980, the chief executive officers of the three hundred largest American companies had incomes twenty-nine times that of the average manufacturing worker. Ten years later the incomes of the top executives were ninety-three times greater. The income of the average employed American

2. These have been detailed at no slight length in one of the small classics of the age of contentment, *Barbarians at the Gate: The Fall of RJR Nabisco* (New York: Harper and Row, 1990), by Bryan Burrough and John Helyar. Among the lush executive perquisites at stake in the takeover of RJR Nabisco was a whole fleet — called the Air Force — of executive jet aircraft, complete with company hangar.

In 1991, two leading business magazines, *Forbes* and *Fortune*, highlighted and, indeed, criticized — *Forbes* in particular — the growth in executive compensation. The reporting was especially poignant in the case of *Fortune*, for the most successful effort at personal profit maximization, there identified as a total reward of $39,060,000 for the year 1990, was that of Steven J. Ross, the head of Time Warner, owner, among other properties, of *Fortune* itself. A co-executive of the same corporation, Nicholas J. Nicholas, also received well up in the millions that year. Some 258 out of 800 chief executives of other firms had annual revenues in excess of a million dollars, giving a new meaning to the old word *millionaire*.

declined slightly in those years.[3] It was these ample and self-endowed returns and the prestige and power associated with high managerial position that attracted, not surprisingly, the interest and obtrusive attention of those who, also not surprisingly, would prefer to have them for themselves. Thus came about two of the most spectacular financial developments of the 1980s: the corporate raids, as they were called, to gain the power and rewards of management, and the buyouts by management seeking to preserve its own position and income. Both were accomplished in essentially the same way — by the borrowing of money against the eventual credit of the corporation to buy up stock from the hitherto passive and languid stockholders.

It would be hard to imagine an economically and socially more damaging design. Both exercises loaded a heavy debt on the firm; interest on this debt then had prior claim over investment in new and improved plant, new products and research and development. In the case of the largest and most egregiously self-serving of the leveraged buyouts, that just mentioned of RJR Nabisco in 1989, heavy losses followed in the immediately ensuing period,[4] and capital spending was slashed sharply in 1990. A Canadian real estate adventurer, Robert Campeau, moving in on some of the biggest and most suc-

3. Benjamin M. Friedman, "Reagan Lives!" *New York Review of Books*, December 20, 1990.
4. *The New York Times*, February 6, 1990. The full story of this dementia is in *Barbarians at the Gate*.

cessful American retail chains, including Bloomingdale's and Federated Department Stores, left them in bankruptcy and briefly, it was said, in some doubt as to whether funds could be found to finance the future acquisition of the goods they were to sell.

After a takeover or buyout, there was often a forced sale of some parts of the firm, frequently the most promising or profitable, to reduce debt and meet interest charges. The high interest charges then kept the firm vulnerable in the event of any individual or general decline in revenues. Notoriously, there were, as well, large, wholly nonfunctional costs for legal, underwriting and financial guidance.[5]

Perhaps the worst financial devastation has been that of the nation's airlines. Here an ill-considered deregulation — faith once again in the market in a public-service industry where utility regulation is normal — has been combined with corporate raiding and leveraged buyouts on an impressive scale. The results have been heavy debt, the bankruptcy of several of the larger airlines, the folding up of Eastern Airlines and of Pan Am, a chaotic muddle

---

5. While RJR Nabisco was the best celebrated example of the corporate-takeover, leveraged-buyout mania, the classically damaging case could have been that of Morgan Stanley and Company, an avowedly conservative investment banking firm, and the takeover of Burlington Industries, the large textile complex. Morgan Stanley extracted in fees and a special dividend an estimated $176 million from Burlington, and the latter was left under an enormous load of debt with "some of its core operations, like its research department, . . . chopped to pieces by cost-cutting drives," and with a large issue of junk bonds trading for a fraction of their original value. *The Wall Street Journal* (December 14, 1990) dealt at length with this case, and the quotation is from its report.

of fares and available routes, an inability to replace aging equipment and, in the end, quite possibly an exploitative monopoly by the survivors.

There were further adverse effects of the mergers and acquisitions mania. These included the socially sterile rewards received by those who traded with inside information on the offers to be made for a specific stock. And there were the losses, in some instances perhaps salutary, of those who were attracted by the prospect of high return and who bought the securities, principally the high-risk, high-interest junk bonds, that financed the operations and that went eventually to discount or default as the full consequences of the aberration became evident. From these losses there was further effect on productive investment and, at least marginally, on consumer spending and the functioning of the economy as a whole. With all else, in the oldest tradition of economic life, the mentally vulnerable, those at one time more obtrusively denoted as fools, were separated, as so often before, from their money.

Yet all was wholly plausible, given the corporate structure and the approved profit-maximizing motivation of the system. All, to repeat, was under the benign cloak of laissez faire and the market.

Legislative or executive action to limit or minimize the destruction — for example, holding hearings to require the approval on economic grounds of the regulatory agency for any large-scale substitution of debt for equity — went all but unmentioned. And such mention would have been met, in any case, with rejection verging on indignation and ridicule. The free enterprise system fully embraces the right to inflict limitless damage on itself.

The mergers and acquisitions mania was, without doubt, the most striking exercise in self-destruction of the culture of contentment. There have, however, been two other highly visible manifestations of this deeply inborn tendency.

The first of these was the real estate speculation of the 1980s, centering on commercial office space in the cities, but extending out to expensive dwellings, in particular condominiums, in the suburbs and resort areas and going on to architecturally questionable skyscrapers in New York City and admittedly hideous gambling casinos in Atlantic City.

As ever, the admiration for the imagination, initiative and entrepreneurship here displayed was extreme. Of those receiving the most self- and public adulation, the premier figure was Donald Trump, briefly and by his own effort and admission the most prestigious economic figure of the time.

The admiration extended to, and into, the nation's biggest banks. Here the loans were large and potentially dangerous, and so, in the nature and logic of modern banking, they were handled with the least care and discretion. The security of the small borrower is traditionally examined with relentless attention; the claims of the large borrower go to the top, where, because of the enormous amounts involved, there is an assumption of especially acute intelligence. The man or woman who borrows $10,000 or $50,000 is seen as a person of average intelligence to be dealt with accordingly. The one who borrows a million or a hundred million is endowed with a presumption of financial genius that provides considerable protection from any unduly vigorous scrutiny. This individual deals with the very senior officers of the bank or financial institution; the prestige of high bureaucratic position means that any lesser officer will be reluctant, perhaps fearing personal career damage, to challenge the ultimate decision. In plausible consequence, the worst errors in banking are regularly made in the largest amount by the highest officials. So it was in the great real estate boom of the age of contentment.

Here the self-destructive nature of the system, if more diffused than in the case of the mergers, acquisitions and leveraged buyouts mania, was greater in eventual economic impact. Excessive acreages of unused buildings, commercial and residential, were created. The need for such construction, given the space demands of the modern business bureaucracy, was believed to be without limit. In later consequence, the solvency of numerous banks, including that of some of the nation's largest and most prestigious institutions, was either fatally impaired or placed in doubt. The lending of both those that failed or were endangered and others was subject, by fear and example, to curtailment. The construction industry was severely constrained and its workers left unemployed. A general recession ensued. Any early warning as to what was happening would have been exceptionally ill received, seen as yet another invasion of the benign rule of laissez faire and a specific interference with the market.

However, in keeping with the exceptions to this rule, there could be eventual salvation in a government bailout of the banks. Insurance of bank deposits — a far from slight contribution to contentment — was permissible, as well as the assurance that were a bank large enough, it would not be allowed to fail. A preventive role by government was not allowed; eventual government rescue was highly acceptable.

Ranking with the real estate and banking aberration was the best publicized of the exercises in financial devastation: the collapse of the savings and loan associations, or, in common parlance, the S&L scandal. This, which was allowed to develop in the 1980s, had emerged by the end of that decade as the largest and costliest venture in public misfeasance, malfeasance and larceny of all time.

Again the basic principle was impressively evident and pursued: laissez faire combined with faith in the benignity of market enterprise. The short-run view took precedence over the more distant consequences. And there was an infinitely vast and obligatory public intervention as those consequences became known.

Starting well back in the last century, the savings and loan associations, under various names, played a small, worthy and largely anonymous role in the American economy. Attracting for deposit the savings of the local community, they then made these available in the form of home loans to the immediately adjacent citizenry. There was strict regulation by federal and state governments as to the interest they could pay and charge and the purpose for which they could make loans. Home ownership being a well-established social good, the S&Ls were eventually given public encouragement and support in the form of a modest government guarantee of their depositors' funds.

Then, with the age and culture of contentment, there came the new overriding commitment to laissez faire and the market and the resulting movement toward general deregulation. The commercial banks, once released from regulation, greatly increased the interest rates there available to depositors, which meant that if the similarly deregulated S&Ls were to compete, they would need to pay higher rates to *their* depositors. Sadly, however, these payments would have to be met by the low rates then in place on a large and passive inventory of earlier mortgage loans. The highly improvident solution was to accord the S&Ls freedom to set rates of interest on the insured deposits and then to go beyond home loans to the widest range of other investments, or what were imaginatively so designated. Also, faithful to principle, government action in the interest of contentment was not curtailed. Instead, the once modest insurance of deposits by the federal government was raised to $100,000 on each S&L

account. The selective view of the role of the state was never more evident.

The foregoing changes were variously enacted or instituted mainly in the early 1980s. They set the stage for what was by far the most feckless and felonious disposition of what, essentially, were public funds in the nation's history, perhaps in any modern nation's history. Deposits guaranteed by the federal government and thus having behind them the full faith and credit of the government were brokered across the country to find the highest rate of return. Such interest was, normally, offered by the institutions most given to irresponsible or larcenous employment of the funds involved. Efforts at correction or restraint, palpably small, were deliberately restricted as being inconsistent with the broad commitment to deregulation.[6] Those still subject to the skeletal and ineffective regulation took their case, not without success, to the Congress. Funds from the publicly guaranteed deposits were thus recycled back to support congressional races in an innovative, if perverse, step toward the public financing of electoral campaigns.

In the latter years of the 1980s, the whole S&L experience came explosively to an end in the first and, in many respects, most dramatic exposure of the public principles

---

6. This inconsistency was made explicit by Secretary of the Treasury Donald Regan, a decisive figure in the debacle. Mr. Regan is thought to have emerged from this service, as later from his service in the White House, as one of the more expendable political figures of the time.

implicit in the age of contentment. The prospective cost, perhaps $2,000 for each American citizen were it equally assessed, was regarded as impressive. Less impressive, perhaps, was the understanding of what underlay the debacle. Here, first of all, was the general commitment to laissez faire, the specific commitment to the market, which had led to the deregulation. But here too was the highly selective character of that commitment. As far as the culture of contentment was concerned, responsibility to find a solution for the shortfall remained firmly with the state. The depositors, large and small — the comfortable rentier community — were at risk; thus the necessity for the continuing role of the government. The whole S&L scandal was, to repeat, one of the clearest displays of the controlling principles of contentment, and certainly it was the most immediately costly.

6

The Bureaucratic Syndrome

*Thought for many is hard work, which is why
it often commands high pay. It also, alas,
is compulsively delegated.*

N O ONE should be in doubt: one of the inescapable features of life in the late twentieth century
is the great, complicated and multilayered organization. With all else, it is the source of much present-
day innovation. The latter is no longer the distinctive
product of one acutely inspired brain, although this source
of invention is still celebrated; normally it is the result
of the cooperative effort of diversely competent specialists, each making his or her uniquely qualified contribution to the common goal. As economic and public
operations become more complex, it is necessary to unite
varying skills, different experience, different education,
resulting specialization and different degrees of intelligence, or, at a minimum, its confident outward expression.

Out of this need for both number and diversity of talents

comes the need for supervision, coordination and command. This, in turn, and depending on the size and complexity of the job at hand, can involve numerous levels of authority, or what is so described. Further, since the requisite knowledge and intelligence derive in large measure from those whose contributions are brought together and coordinated, so in no slight measure does the power in the organization. The modern corporation or public agency has an internal intelligence and authority of its own; these are to some extent independent of, or superior to, those of the persons who are seen, and who see themselves, as in command. The latter point should not go unremarked. The power attributed to the cabinet secretary recently arrived in office with no previous experience in his or her now-assigned task or to the corporate chief executive officer now rewarded for an orderly and disciplined performance in the ranks is subject to an exaggeration to which those so celebrated happily and even diligently contribute.

Not surprisingly, the culture of the great organization is enormously influenced by the pursuit of contentment. This is evident in two important ways, both proceeding from the discomforts associated with original or dissenting thought. Also involved is a deeply ingrained, much invoked distinction between private organization and public organization — between the great private bureaucracy and its large public counterpart. In the culture of contentment the former is perceived as efficient and dynamic, while the latter is thought to be mentally moribund, seriously incompetent and, on frequent occasion, offensively arrogant.

In any large organization there must, first of all, be a well-developed sense of common purpose. This is informally, and sometimes formally, articulated in the large modern firm as company policy; in the public organization it is called official or departmental policy. "We are committed this year to big, if somewhat less fuel-efficient cars; that is what the American customer wants." "The Communist threat may no longer exist, but our policy still calls for a strong defense."

Individual contentment, all are aware, is powerfully served by acceptance of this formally stated or commonly assumed purpose. Resistance or dissent is adverse to the cooperative effort essential to organizational success. Accordingly, the man or woman who, however justly, questions the established policy is challenging one of the basic requirements of organized achievement. That requirement is to accept and serve the common goal — to be, in common terminology, a good team player. Needless to say, that is also the course that contributes to personal comfort. Few things are so agreeable, Tolstoy observed, as to surrender one's self to the regiment. Few things are so discomfiting, even painful, as the cerebration and resulting speech or action that impair one's social and working relationships, and nothing can be so damaging to prospects for pay and promotion. "The fellow may be bright enough, but he is not cooperative."

However, that is by no means all. It is part of the human vanity that there is intrinsic reward in mental effort. For some, doubtless, this is true; for most, mental effort is something that it is exceptionally pleasant to avoid. From this comes the nature of all great organization: those serving it have a powerful commitment to established belief and thus to established action. This regularly rewards those who surrender independent thought to organizational policy. Their surrender, in turn, serves personal acceptance and social harmony and is both central to the culture of contentment and a powerful conditioning therein. The organization man is happy with what exists. As this mood controls his private life, so it controls his public attitude. Nothing so breeds acquiescence in, or indifference to, social shortcoming as daily exposure to the misjudgments, eccentricities and inanities of private organization. With the rise of the great corporation there comes a contented accommodation to the larger errors of public life, and notably those with no immediate effect on the one who observes them.

The second way in which modern organization cultivates acceptance of what comfortably exists in the age of contentment is by diminishing the role of thought itself. Especially in the higher reaches of organization, needed thought is a commitment, perhaps more precisely an intrusion, that is not to be faced but rather to be delegated. Encountering a problem, an organization man turns naturally, automatically, to a subordinate. The latter is told to get on to it. This he then does by turning to an assistant, and the delegation continues. The culture of organization runs strongly to the shifting of problems to others — to an escape from personal mental effort and responsibility. This, in turn, becomes the larger public attitude. It is for others to do the worrying, take the action. In the world of the great organization, problems are not solved but passed on.

And there is a further effect. The delegation process just cited adds ineluctably to the layers of command and to the prestige associated with command. That prestige is regularly measured by the number of the individual's subordinates: "How many people does he have under him?" In consequence, although organization, by its nature, has a deeply static tendency as to action, it is relentlessly dynamic in the multiplication of personnel. In further consequence, the number of those responding to its attitudes and behavior patterns has a strong tendency also to increase. In the private sector of the modern economy the great corporation occupies a steadily more important position — by common calculation, the largest five hundred industrial firms in the United States account for around 60 percent of all production. Within those firms there is an intrinsic dynamic acting to increase what, by broad definition, is called managerial personnel, and with the increase in their numbers there is an increase in those subject influentially to the broad culture of contentment.

This commitment to the culture of contentment is, to repeat, common to all organization. And so are the expansive tendencies that enlarge the numbers so committed. But we come now to a radical difference between public and private organization. The difference turns specifically on the word *bureaucracy*.

The general reference to large organization in public service is to bureaucracy, and the connotation is uniformly adverse. This is especially true in the United States. Those who serve in large governmental agencies or departments are, it is thought, an inferior part of the citizenry. It is recognized that, as individuals, they may be diligent, personable and socially useful. Collectively they are stolid, incompetent and, above all, a burden on the society. They are "bureaucrats."

A vital distinction must, however, be made between those in the public sector who serve the culture and goals of contentment and those whose agencies are seen as a threat. Workers in the departments of government concerned with regulatory activity, tax collection and especially with welfare services have the fully negative reputation of bureaucracy; those so employed are, collectively, intrusive, incompetent and self-serving. In contrast, those in the military establishment, in lesser measure in the Department of State, the CIA and the other intelligence agencies, and notably also in the administration of Social Security are exempt from attack. The term *bureaucracy* is but rarely applied to them and almost never in a condemnatory tone. Those there serving are not bureaucrats and certainly not, in the common expression, "lousy bureaucrats." They are, generally, good and loyal public servants. It will be evident, to repeat, that those agencies and departments of government that serve contentment have a standing in public attitude and expression very different from those that collect taxes, succor the poor or enforce regulations.

The case of the military is especially to be remarked. None can doubt that the Pentagon and its civilian and military components conform in an exceptionally rigorous way to the bureaucratic mode. Policy is there proclaimed and accepted as a matter of course; thought and resulting independent action are fully surrendered. There is a surprised reaction to the occasional independent expression — to the whistle-blower. That there is overmanning is not in doubt; in past times those who were faced with workless days and weeks in the Department of Defense described themselves as suffering from Pentagonorrhea. Yet the military establishment is almost entirely exempt from the adverse attitudes reserved for, say, the urban welfare bureaucracy, that which attends the highly urgent needs of the functional underclass. The civilian and especially the uniformed personnel who make up the military power are enthusiastically hailed for their service to their country. There is no similar admiration or celebration of those who, often at greater personal danger, render assistance to the poor in the inner-city slums.

The lesson for anyone contemplating a public career is evident. Service to national defense, to foreign relations, even to the CIA, ensures public esteem. That will be the reward from public activities that are consistent with the culture of contentment. A modest glow attaches also to anyone administering or defending pensions for the old or price and income supports for often affluent farmers. There will be no like repute from dispensing aid to families with dependent children or awarding food stamps. Here, alas, one will be a bureaucrat.

There is, perhaps, a more substantive difference to be noted between the public servant and the bureaucrat. The former is heard with respect when he or she asks for public moneys; the latter's requests are simply a burden.

The most comprehensive escape from the adverse reputation of bureaucracy, however, is found in the private sector and is reserved for those who occupy the upper ranks of the large modern corporation. Their immunity from criticism is central, even vital, to the culture of contentment. This calls for a special word.

That the large and complex business enterprise is an essential feature of modern economic life has been sufficiently noted.[1] In past times the mental sclerosis asso-

---

1. I have dealt with this in detail in *The New Industrial State* (Boston: Houghton Mifflin, 1967, and later editions). I there referred to those making up the organization, and particularly those concerned with innovation, as the technostructure, a term that has gained some currency.

ciated with bureaucracy, especially in those firms that are seemingly exempt from the pressures of technological change or shifting consumer fashion, has been greatly evident and, indeed, has been much remarked. That condition in the coal and the steel industries, and particularly in the once industrially dominant United States Steel Corporation, is a well-read chapter in American economic history. The history of like enterprises in Britain and on the Continent is similar. The General Motors Corporation and, in lesser measure, the other automobile companies in the United States are now held to have a corporate culture that verges dangerously on desuetude. From this has come, at least in part, their diminished position in American and world markets.

The more visible and compelling evidence of the bureaucratic tendency in the large corporation is reported daily in the financial press, and especially when there is any softening of markets. The corporation is then described as "shedding" personnel, meaning, notably, those in the managerial or bureaucratic ranks. (From the corporate bureaucracy members are never discharged, fired or sacked, only shed.) From larger enterprises the number so dispensed with runs frequently to the thousands.

The shedding, in all normal comment, is taken as a move to lower costs and achieve greater efficiency. The virtually unasked question is what the people thus and so routinely let go were doing in the first place. Their removal is, indeed, compelling proof of the unchecked bureaucratic propensity to multiply personnel — the bureaucratic urge to delegate problem-solving and requisite thought and to enhance personal prestige by increasing the number of one's subordinates.

Nonetheless, the large private corporation is generally exempt from the adverse implications of bureaucracy. It is not a bureaucracy but an enterprise. Those who work in it are executives, engineers, marketing specialists, advertising or public relations experts, but never or almost never bureaucrats. As in the case of the members of the military establishment or the State Department, this is an exemption that the organization men (and some women) of the great corporation are all but automatically accorded in the age of contentment.

Three concepts that contribute to the immunity of the large corporation and its management from the adverse implications of bureaucracy may be noted. It is said, first, that, unlike the public organization, the corporation is subject to the discipline of the market. The recurrent accumulation and shedding of personnel show, however, that this is not a force of undeviating rigor. Nor does formal economics in this world of imperfect competition hold such restraint to be especially severe. The often more than ample compensation that regularly accrues to the senior executives and is sanctioned by acquiescent management-appointed directors is further evidence of the elasticity of market discipline. It could be that the appropriation of public funds within which the public agency lives is, on occasion, more confining.

Also serving the disguise of the bureaucratic tendency in the modern private corporation and its leadership is the concept and vision of the entrepreneur. Original, self-motivated, innovative, welcoming risk, an executive so described is a creature of the market, the market he himself, in the frequent case, is assumed to have discovered. The entrepreneur is the economist's greatest hero, a role celebrated by one of the discipline's most noted figures, Joseph Alois Schumpeter.[2] Here is the source, the dynamism, of economic progress. With the much revered classical entrepreneur the executives of the great corporation are accorded an honorary, if otherwise improbable, association. The head of the large business enterprise rejoices in so seeing himself and in being so seen.

His counterpart, in fact, is the army general operating with a large and compliant staff far behind the lines, who pictures himself as leading the tanks in fierce and unrelenting combat. In the early days of the great American S&L scandal, the principal official of the regulatory authority involved spoke in exculpatory terms of Charles Keating, the most notorious figure in this concerted attack on the public interest and pocketbook. He was, it was said, a "very entrepreneurial businessman."[3] An entrepreneur can, indeed, fail, but he can do no wrong.

So it is inevitable that the heads of General Motors,

2. The author, most memorably, of *The Theory of Economic Development: An Inquiry into Profits, Capital, Credit, Interest, and the Business Cycle* (Cambridge: Harvard University Press, 1934).

3. *The Wall Street Journal*, November 22, 1989.

General Electric, Citibank and Shell, having made their way up through a bureaucracy, wish to believe that they too are entrepreneurs. Thus they gain exemption from the taint of bureaucracy, for no entrepreneur is a bureaucrat.

Finally, the great enterprise — the large modern corporation — is extensively under the protection of conventional economic education. This is still strongly oriented to the competitive market, which is populated, of necessity, by numerous small operators — the entrepreneurs again — or, if more exceptionally, by larger monopolists and oligopolists who are also fully committed to profit maximization for the firm. The bureaucratic tendency and the particular motivation of the organization men are not explored. That such tendency and such motivation exist most economists would agree, but these do not lend themselves to the geometry and equations of formal theory. They are not thought to belong in economic instruction. And perhaps there is another reason they are not more recognized: bureaucratic lethargy and incompetence would not be pleasant to teach; to do so could lead only to disturbing questions.

The inhabitants of the modern great organization, public and private, are, as we have seen, strongly conditioned to the culture of contentment. However, the relationship, as the preceding pages suggest, is complex. All are bureaucrats, but this term is reserved for those in public life who serve in organizations inimical or thought to be in-

imical to private contentment. Those in more accommodating roles are public servants or, on occasion, heroes
of the Republic. And there is marked reluctance on the
part of the members of the great private organization to
accept the designation of "bureaucrat." Subordination of
the corporation to the market, the heroic mantle of the
entrepreneur and the tenets of conventional economic
education are all cited or used to diminish this resem-
blance. That the culture of contentment with its passive
acceptance of short-run comfort is the ruling force in modern large-scale organization and in the great bureaucracy
cannot, one ventures, be thought seriously in question.

7

The Economic Accommodation, I

*Economists regularly engage in political theory,
masking normative judgments with
seemingly objective analysis.*
— CONRAD P. WALIGORSKI

O NE of the most reliable, though not necessarily
most distinguished, accomplishments of economics is its ability to accommodate its view
of economic process, instruction therein and recom-
mended public action to specific economic and political
interest. Craftsmen, sometimes of no slight ability, are
regularly available for this service.

In the first half of the last century, the age of burgeoning capitalism, David Ricardo and the Reverend Thomas
Robert Malthus, the two most influential economic
voices of those years, saw an industrial world in which a
handful of exceedingly well maintained and powerful
capitalists dominated society from the dark satanic mills.
In those mills thousands, not excluding small children,
labored without power and for the pittance that allowed

only for a sadly limited existence. As I have indicated on other occasions, it would be hard to design a better cover for this far from compassionate economic and social order than that which Ricardo and Malthus provided. Wages, they held, were pressed ineluctably to the margin of subsistence by natural law — and specifically, as Malthus especially urged, by the natural law of procreation, this being the uncontrollable breeding habits of the human species. From the force of the growing population and the resulting very natural competition for jobs, wages were thus brought down to the minimum necessary for survival.

Malthus, a compassionate man, did not think this grievous tendency wholly without remedy; ministers in the wedding ceremony should, he thought, warn against unduly prodigious intercourse. Until this family planning design became effective, however, the mill owner and the capitalist could find comfort in a condition not of their own making. They could react with indignation to any thought of trade union or government intervention, however improbable, for that contravened the natural — and sexual — order.

Not less accommodating, then as now, was the social commitment to laissez faire, the doctrine that is thought to have emerged in seventeenth-century France, although its actual origins are debated. This, as already noted, is the belief that economic life has within itself the capacity to solve its own problems and for all to work out for the best in the end.

In Britain in its age of industrial triumph nothing was more helpful than the support given by all accepted economic theory to free trade. This was urged both eloquently and elegantly by Adam Smith. Here the accommodation was especially clear. For Britain, the industrially most advanced of countries, free trade was of obvious advantage, and, like laissez faire, it acquired a strong theological aura. In Germany and the United States, on the other hand, economic interest was better served by tariffs. Accordingly, the most respected economists in those countries — the noted Friedrich List in Germany, the eloquent Henry Carey in the United States — spoke vigorously for protection for their national "infant industries," protection, in fact, from the products of the British colossus.

Such was the service of economics to early capitalism. And such service has continued. Toward the end of the last century, in what has now come down to us as the Gilded Age, Herbert Spencer avowed the economic and social doctrine of the survival of the fittest — it is to him and not to Darwin that we owe those words. Though British, Spencer was a figure of heroic proportions in the United States, as were his disciples. His most distinguished acolyte, William Graham Sumner of Yale, served the gilded constituency in remarkably explicit language: "The millionaires are a product of natural selection. . . . They may fairly be regarded as the naturally selected agents of society for certain work. They get high wages and live in luxury, but the bargain is a good one for society."[1]

Thorstein Veblen, who, oddly, was one of Sumner's students, did, it must be said, acquire even greater fame for his inconvenient treatment of this doctrine. The rich and the powerful he saw in anthropological terms — their habits of life were those of tribal leaders; their enjoyments, tribal rites — and he so described them.[2]

In this century, for as long as the dominant industrial and financial mood was opposed to the New Deal, so, as I have already indicated, were the most reputable economists. They cited its conflict with free market principles, its impairment of essential economic motivation and, above all, its seeming subversion of sound money and public finance. Economists who approved or served the New Deal were scorned in no slight measure for their dissidence and even their eccentricity. Only when the basic ideas won acceptance did economists in general step forward to give their approval.

I come now to the modern accommodation of economics to contentment. This is at two levels. There is, first,

1. William Graham Sumner, *The Challenge of Facts and Other Essays,* edited by Albert Galloway Keller (New Haven: Yale University Press, 1914), p. 90.
2. His academic fame came also from the reaction of the presidents of the institutions in which he taught. They, on becoming acquainted, however reluctantly, with his views and with the grave discontent they caused to college trustees and the adjacent business community, found it wise to have him move elsewhere.

the accepted economics strongly represented in the textbooks, in normal economic discourse and in established
belief. And there is, second, that which has been rather
specifically designed to serve contentment and is widely,
if not quite universally, so recognized.

The reputable accommodation of economics to contentment begins with the broad commitment to the doctrine,
more often called the principle, of laissez faire; of this,
ample mention has been made. In keeping therewith, government intervention, specifically government regulation, is unnecessary and normally damaging to the beneficent processes of nature. Or, since things will work out
in the long run, it is an expression of impatience.

Accordingly, the overwhelming presumption as to the
necessity for government action is negative. The case for
any specific intervention must be strongly proved; the
case against rests not on empirical demonstration, not
alone on formal theory, but also on deeper theological
grounds. As you must have faith in God, you must have
faith in the system; to some extent the two are identical.

Over the centuries this faith has, indeed, been subject
to waves of strength and weakness. In the age of contentment, not surprisingly, it is strong. Perhaps more than
any other belief, it has been a sustaining force for the
contented. It supports the powerful commitment to the
short run and to the rejection of longer-run concerns. (In
ultimate support, of course, is the most quoted observa-

tion by John Maynard Keynes: "In the long run we are all dead.")

The modern commitment to laissez faire is not, however, without exception. There are, as sufficiently indicated in earlier chapters, forms of state action that are considered firmly in the service of contentment. The rescue of failing banks and other financial institutions is an obvious case, as also support to the military establishment — anciently, the defense of the realm. So also publicly provided pensions for the more comfortable of the aged. And there are exceptions for numerous lesser matters. Laissez faire is a general but not a confining force in the culture of contentment.

To other, more specific and no less self-serving economic accommodation I now turn. The doctrines that have been more obviously designed to support contentment are discussed in the next chapter.

The most serious general threat to contentment results, perhaps needless to say, from the intrinsic tendency of capitalism to instability — to recession or depression, with its adverse effect not alone on employment but also on income and profit, and to the very real fear of inflation.

Since the Great Depression of the 1930s, there has been a broad consensus that the government must take steps to mitigate or control these manifestations of instability. It must have a macroeconomic policy for economic stabilization and expansion. This agreement is not quite absolute; an onset of recession in the economy invariably brings predictions from economists that it will be short and self-correcting. Here again the theology of benign result: the business cycle has its own beneficent dynamic. Nonetheless, some public action is now generally deemed necessary, and the more basic accommodation to contentment lies in the specifics of that action. Reduced to their essentials, they are rather simple and even obvious. Limiting popular understanding of them, however, is a covering cloak of highly functional mystification that admirably serves the culture of contentment.

The basic feature of a recession or depression is a reduction, for whatever reason, in the flow of effective demand — of purchasing power — for capital goods and for consumer goods and services. The result is a shrinkage of production and employment and a cumulative effect as corporations and consumers find their purchasing power diminished and they react accordingly.

The causes of inflation are not quite symmetrically the opposite. Inflation comes when, for whatever reason, the flow of demand or purchasing power presses on a significant number of goods and services, allowing or forcing a general upward movement in prices. Additionally in the case of inflation, however, powerful microeconomic factors, as they are called, may force producers to raise prices over a substantial part of the economy. Wage negotiations leading to higher costs and forcing higher prices or, a more spectacular case in recent times, a large increase in oil

84

and energy prices may have a strong inflationary effect.

There are for economists a professionally rewarding number of causes of the forces leading to the curtailment of demand that induces recession or depression, or of those initiating an expansion of demand. Perhaps there may be a broad, causally undefined tendency for consumers to spend more or less or for producers to invest more or less. Waves of optimism and pessimism have an ancient and well-avowed role in the economics of the business cycle. There is the effect of the fear that follows the collapse of speculative episodes or other banking or financial crises, and the effect of increases or reductions in export demand.

Yet other factors can also be important. Much action, however, is beyond the range of the favored public policy. Public oratory designed to restore consumer confidence and influence business investment, for example, though much employed, is not known to be especially useful. In the early years of the Great Depression presidential assurances of the certain imminence of recovery were thought to be a sign of a more serious prospect. Thus they had an adverse influence on the securities markets and, it was thought, on business confidence.[3] In the painful recession of the early 1990s, as this is written, similar oratory emanates from Washington on a daily basis.

In fact, useful action against recession or inflation

---

3. I have dealt with this in *The Great Crash, 1929* (Boston: Houghton Mifflin, 1955, and later editions).

comes down to government measures to expand or to contract the flow of consumer and investment spending. Action against inflation also may involve a general restraint on costs, notably wage or, on occasion, energy costs, as these may force up prices over a wide area of economic activity. The relevant choices are fiscal policy, monetary policy and a policy as regards wages or other influential costs as these put upward pressure on prices. The one that conforms most agreeably to the controlling principles of contentment is wonderfully clear. It is the one that, not surprisingly, has the most general economic approval.

Fiscal policy involves action to increase or decrease the flow of spending — of effective demand — by adding to or subtracting from the government contribution thereto. This is accomplished by increasing or decreasing government spending, taxes remaining the same, or by increasing or decreasing taxes, expenditures remaining the same. Or it is accomplished by infinitely varied combinations of such actions.

Fiscal policy does enjoy a certain standing in established economic discussion and instruction. As earlier observed, however, it accords very badly with the controlling tenets of contentment, for it means, needless to say, an enlarged role for government. Also, a deliberate increase in taxes to limit the flow of spending and mitigate inflation is out of the question; resistance to taxes for whatever reason is basic in the culture of contentment.

Equally impossible is an increase in public spending to add to the flow of purchasing power unless it serves military or other authorized purpose.

A reduction in spending as an anti-inflation measure is commended in principle but is subject to the controlling role of the needed expenditure. A reduction in taxes is similarly possible, but, as will presently be seen, tax reduction is held to have diffcrent and justifying factors of its own that are unrelated to the business cycle.

Large and persistent public deficits substantially supporting the flow of private expenditure were accepted, if rhetorically regretted, during the 1980s, and they continue. However, the deliberate management of expenditures and taxes for economic support or restraint was not acceptable. In the years of President Ronald Reagan there was a strong suggestion from numerous economists that such action was historically obsolete. It belonged to the departed age of John Maynard Keynes; time had passed it by.

Before considering the second line of government intervention, monetary policy, there is a third and less often used instrument of economic management. That is direct restraint on costs, and more particularly wage-costs, as these may force up prices and cause inflation. This design is under an especially stringent economic ban in the age of contentment, and peculiarly so in the English-speaking countries. In Germany, Japan, Austria, Switzerland and Scandinavia, wages are negotiated within the limits of what can be paid at the existing level of prices; this is commonplace policy. Although enjoying a certain respectability in the United States in past times — in World War II, the Korean War, informally under John F. Kennedy and notably in a general freeze of wages and prices by Richard Nixon in 1971 — wage and price controls are now considered an unthinkable extension of government authority. Even steps to restrain energy costs and to conserve use are beyond the pale. The former intrudes on an area where the market is authoritative and, as ever, ultimately benign. The latter — conservation — lies under the general proscription on action for long-run effect.

For practical purposes, only the second of the major lines of government action against inflation and recession is consistent with the tenets of contentment. That is monetary policy, and here the economic accommodation is nearly complete.

As the preferred choice, monetary policy is not just a residual, however; it has strong affirmative values that are specifically in keeping with the controlling principles of contentment. Of these I have made previous mention; to them in more detail I now turn.

Commending monetary policy in the age of contentment is, first, the element of mystification strongly associated with money and its management, something that economists over the years have done little to dissipate. One of the cherished distinctions of the economist is the public belief that he or she has privileged access to the assumed mystery of money. To some extent the great banker or other financier enjoys the same distinction, at least until, in the not infrequent case, some large error of speculative optimism is grievously exposed.

Here we must differentiate between monetary policy and what is called monetarism. The first refers generally to any action by a central bank to control the volume of borrowing and lending by commercial banks with effects that will presently be noted. Monetarism, a more specific and imaginative doctrine, the eloquent and diligent spokesman of which is Professor Milton Friedman in the United States, focuses all economic policy on the total supply of money in circulation — cash, bank deposits, whatever buys goods and pays bills. It holds that if this total is tightly controlled and allowed to increase only as the economy expands, prices will be stable and the economy will function well out of its own independent strength.

At one time monetarism had a prominent role in the political economy of contentment. A better design to limit the role of government and to support the view that all economic life would function under its own automatic guidance could hardly be imagined. Alas, however, the monetarist faith was unduly optimistic even for the contented. A rigorous effort at monetary control in the early 1980s in the United States contributed to the most severe recession since the Great Depression. Union power and resulting upward pressure on prices were, indeed, curbed, but this, in considerable part, was done by curbing the economic strength and even solvency of employers. Monetarism did not quite die after this debacle; it was, however, relegated to the economic shadows, where it remains.

When one comes to the more prosaic world of monetary policy as it affects prices and economic activity, the mystery and magic disappear, and rather completely, on examination. The practical effect of monetary action on the economy, as earlier indicated, is ultimately through a substantial control of interest rates. By raising or lowering the cost of borrowing by its member banks, the Federal Reserve in the United States, like central banks in other countries, has a substantial, if clearly imperfect, measure of control over the rates at which commercial banks and other financial institutions can lend money to their customers. From this comes the economic effect.

Higher interest rates discourage consumer borrowing and expenditure for home ownership and consumer durable goods, and they are presumed to discourage investment and associated spending by business enterprises. From this come the restrictive effect on total spending in the economy — on aggregate demand — and ultimately the control of inflation. The opposite policy, a resort to lower interest rates, less costly borrowing, is taken to have the reverse effect. Here, appropriately demystified, is monetary policy.

Anciently economists have, indeed, questioned the symmetry of this process: the metaphor used is that one can pull an object along the floor with a string, but, alas, one cannot shove it along with a string. Monetary policy can pull economic activity down; it cannot so assuredly shove it up. By those economists committed to monetary policy and the many who watch their actions with awe, this is not thought a compelling disqualification.

That monetary policy, with its wide economic approval, stands solidly in the service of contentment is not in doubt, for it involves virtually no government apparatus, the insignificant bureaucratic establishment of the central bank apart. The Federal Reserve System in the United States is accorded exemption by law from both legislative and executive authority; it is independent. This independence, it is accepted, is subject to presidential and other public pressures, and it is more specifically compromised by an intimate and statutory relationship with the commercial banks and less formally with the financial community as a whole. The latter have the accepted right to pass public judgment on central-bank policy, and no Federal Reserve chairman would be thought acceptable were he subject to severe criticism from the banking world. In actual practice, no such criticism is ever thought deserved.

The financial community finds explicit satisfaction in an active central-bank policy. It sets high store by preventing inflation, and in the larger culture of contentment inflation is more to be feared, on balance, than unemployment. It has an especially strong commitment to interest rates that more than compensate for the rate of inflation, and it also seeks to have the central bank move strongly against inflation — more strongly than against recession. The asymmetry in attitude here, while little emphasized in the age of contentment, is notably real.

High interest rates, as earlier mentioned, reward with income a very considerable and very influential part of the community of contentment. In the accepted economic attitudes, however, central-bank policy is socially neutral. In fact, and as earlier noted, it strongly favors the rentier class, a group that is both affluent and vocal. It is an indubitably inescapable fact that those who have money to lend are likely to have more money than those who do not have money to lend — an economic truth that stands on a par with the unimpeachable observation attributed to Calvin Coolidge that when many people are out of work, unemployment results. In the 1980s, personal income derived from interest payments increased from $272 billion to $681 billion, or by 150 percent. Income from wage payments increased by 97 percent.

And there is further affirmation. The 1980s were years of large and persistent deficits in the budget of the United States. These did not escape notice or criticism. On the other hand, the high interest rates by which inflation was kept under control invited little adverse comment, the reason being that they were much enjoyed by the recipients, were wholly in keeping with the mood of contentment, and thus again, and sadly, were economically acceptable.

*

There is, of course, a downside to all this. As has been indicated, high interest rates, the inevitable counterpart of an active monetary policy and especially of one in combination, as in the 1980s, with a soft budget or fiscal policy, act against inflation by discouraging business borrowing and investment. And they act similarly against consumer borrowing and expenditure. Business borrowing is generally for new and improved plant and equipment; that by consumers is in substantial measure for housing. It follows that a prime effect of an active monetary policy is to discourage investment for improved economic performance and for housing construction. In the longer run, less efficient, less competitive industry, a shortage of housing and homelessness, are (and have been) the inevitable result. This, however, is not prominent in established economic discussion.

There have also, in the recent past, been other effects. The deficit in the public accounts has meant that interest charges make up an increasing share of the budget. Also, the high real interest rates have attracted funds from abroad, and from the resulting conversion of other currencies into dollars have come an artificially high rate of exchange for the latter, a strong resulting bonus to imports and, in parallel, an adverse price for exports. The resulting trade deficit has changed the United States from being the world's largest creditor to being, without a close contender, its greatest debtor. From this has come an important effect on the availability of money for overseas use, one of the two pillars of foreign policy — a matter to be noted presently. But the higher budget costs of interest and the effect on the nation's foreign position and policy were the consequences in the longer run, and, as sufficiently observed, what happens in the long run the culture of contentment traditionally ignores. To this too the established economics accommodates. There is satisfaction of a sort in finding in this culture and its attitudes a compelling consistency.

8

The Economic Accommodation, II

S HAS BEEN NOTED in the last chapter, reputable or, as it is often called, mainstream economics has for some centuries given grace and acceptability to convenient belief — to what the socially and economically favored most wish or need to have believed. This economics, to repeat, is wholly reputable; it permeates and even dominates professional discussion and writing, the textbooks and classroom instruction.

This is especially true of one approved element of larger economic policy, namely, monetary policy. It has major scholarly standing as a design for preventing or mitigating inflation and recession or depression, its questionable effectiveness, especially against a diminished flow of demand and recession, notwithstanding. That it is a way of guiding action away from the discomforts of tax and expenditure policy, and also from a wage and price policy;

that it rewards a large and financially influential rentier class; and certainly that it is not economically and socially neutral go unmentioned.

In contrast, there are lines of economic thought and persuasion important to contentment that do not enjoy serious scholarly respect. They have about them an aspect of contrivance — of being concocted after the fact to justify the particular interest or need that they serve. This could be wrong and even unfair; nearly all authors, whatever their service to special interest, however apparent the pecuniary rewards and the applause, are able with slight personal effort to find scholarly virtue and integrity in their own asserted views. So it may be here.

To serve contentment, there were and are three basic requirements. One is the need to defend the general limitation on government as regards the economy; there must be a doctrine that offers a feasible presumption against government intervention. The broad commitment to laissez faire has been sufficiently noted. So also the supporting positions of Ricardo, Malthus and Herbert Spencer. But these names are not widely known, and, in the case of Malthus and Spencer, there is a somewhat adverse connotation; they are not authorities to be readily or wisely cited. A completely reputable and compelling name is needed.

The second, more specific need is to find social justification for the untrammeled, uninhibited pursuit and possession of wealth. This cannot rest in the enjoyment of wealth by the wealthy, undoubted as that enjoyment may be. There is need for demonstration that the pursuit of wealth or even less spectacular well-being serves a serious, even grave social purpose.

Of equal importance here is the need for a justification that does not open an abyss between those who are rich and those who are merely comfortable; otherwise there could be a damaging conflict within the culture of contentment. The case for the rich must seem benign — perhaps essential — to the only comfortably affluent.

The third need is to justify a reduced sense of public responsibility for the poor. Those so situated, the members of the functional and socially immobilized underclass, must, in some very real way, be seen as the architects of their own fate. If not, they could be, however marginally, on the conscience of the comfortable. There could be a disturbing feeling, however fleeting, of unease, even guilt. Why is one so happy while so many struggle to survive — or fail the struggle? This could be psychologically unpleasant and, if carried to extremes through socially compelled charity and philanthropy or, more forcefully, through government action, could result in unwanted personal expense.

To serve these ends, it must be emphasized, the required doctrine need not be subject to serious empirical proof. Or perhaps, as will be noted presently, it need not even be seriously persuasive. It is the availability of an assertable doctrine that is important; it is that availability and not the substance that serves.[1]

The seemingly most available and influential voice for the larger case against unwanted government action, or more specifically that part which is not in the service of contentment, has been Adam Smith. The needed doctrine was presumed to come from his truly memorable *An Inquiry into the Nature and Causes of the Wealth of Nations*, first published in 1776, the year of American independence. Adam Smith is the most widely known name in economics; *Wealth of Nations* remains after two centuries the most widely known title of an economic work. There was, accordingly, a persuasive case for Smith as the voice of the economics of contentment, and he was so chosen. There was here a large measure of contrivance, much of it in relative innocence on the part of those involved. The presidential acolytes in Mr. Reagan's White House wore neckties bearing the picture of the master.[2] They felt and avowed that they were in the service of the true prophet. His controlling role was succinctly expressed: "We're getting back to basics."

1. A point made by Kevin Phillips in *The Politics of Rich and Poor: Wealth and the American Electorate in the Reagan Aftermath* (New York: Random House, 1990). "Conservatives in 1981," he observes, "could not have moved public policy so far merely with a Chamber of Commerce viewpoint. No mere accountant mentality could have popularized a program almost certain to help the rich at the expense of others . . ." (p. 59).

2. See Peggy Noonan, *What I Saw at the Revolution: A Political Life in the Reagan Era* (New York: Random House, 1990).

It is perhaps unfortunate that few, perhaps none, who so cited Adam Smith had read his great book. He was, in reality, the supreme pragmatist and, with much else, was fully open to a necessary or useful role for the state: "Smith's position on the role of the state in a capitalist society was close to that of a modern twentieth century U.S. liberal democrat."[3] Smith was also alarmingly doubtful about some of the more cherished capitalist institutions of our time.

He was unquestionably and effectively in opposition to the mercantilist service of government to the great merchant class, for this had conferred extensive tariff and monopoly privileges on the latter. He wanted freedom of trade, motivated by the universal force of self-interest. This, in turn, he saw as guiding economic life to socially beneficent results — here his famous invisible hand.

However, he was also deeply averse to joint stock companies, now called corporations: "The directors of such companies . . . being the managers rather of other people's money than of their own, it cannot well be expected that they should watch over it with the same anxious vigilance with which the partners in a private copartnery frequently watch over their own. . . . Negligence and profusion, therefore, must always prevail, more or less, in the management of the affairs of such a company."[4] Modern ad-

3. Spencer J. Pack, *Capitalism as a Moral System: Adam Smith's Critique of the Free Market Economy* (Brookfield, Vt.: Edward Elgar, 1991), p. 1.

4. Adam Smith, *Wealth of Nations*, part 3 (New York: P. F. Collier and Son, 1902), p. 112.

vocates of free enterprise would find Smith's attack on corporations deeply disconcerting.

His views on government and government services would be decried as well, for he emphasized that a civilized country has a great many necessary expenses for which there is no need in one that is, as he said, "barbarous." His position on taxation would be equally distressing, for he was greatly attracted by the idea of a proportional wealth tax.

On any recent visit to the United States, Smith the pragmatist would almost certainly have been troubled by the extensive relegation of the central cities to a primitive barbarity. He would have noted with distress that a strong and partly autonomous military power had united industry and government in a manner that, under the mercantilist cognomen, he had astringently deplored. He would have noted how extensively deregulation — the release of industry, commerce and finance from government supervision and intervention — was being pursued in his name. He would have been less than pleased that when it was applied to the savings and loan associations, government ᵢ ⁻ⁿce of deposits had been retained and that this had led on to the licensed use, misuse and larcenous appropriation of what, essentially, were government funds. Here, indeed, was a mercantilist association between the state and private pecuniary accumulation. Smith would have been no strong advocate of the public purposes of the age of contentment. This, to repeat, would have been discovered had he been read. It was, as I have said, perhaps less deliberate contrivance than innocence that brought his name to the support of the political economy of contentment.

For the socially uninhibited pursuit of wealth no classical source, not even Smith, however imaginatively misused, was wholly satisfactory. The problems with Herbert Spencer and William Graham Sumner have been noted in the preceding chapter. Original work, legitimately called invention, was necessary. The most satisfactory of the needed ideas came from George Gilder, a free-lance philosopher whose excellently timed, well-written volume *Wealth and Poverty*[5] acquired near biblical standing in the early 1980s.

With commendable candor, Mr. Gilder called for "the necessity for faith," as opposed to substance, in a chapter forthrightly so entitled. He avowed that "material progress is ineluctably elitist: it makes the rich richer and increases their numbers, exalting a few extraordinary men who can produce wealth over the democratic masses who consume it. . . . Material progress is difficult: it requires from its protagonists long years of diligence and sacrifice, devotion and risk that can be elicited only by high rewards."[6] Finding that the needed faith was unavailable even from the approved economic orthodoxy, Mr. Gilder warned that "material progress is inimical to scientific

5. New York: Basic Books, 1981.
6. Gilder, p. 259.

economics: it cannot be explained or foreseen in mechanistic or mathematical terms."[7]

When speaking of action, he was specific and categorical: "Regressive taxes help the poor."[8] "In order to succeed, the poor need most of all the spur of their poverty."[9]

Questions not emanating from mechanistic or mathematical economics come inevitably to mind. Most modern production, which is to say most material progress, is in the hands of large corporate enterprises; the Fortune 500 corporations, as earlier noted, contribute around 60 percent of all industrial production in the United States. The concept of a corporate genius inspired to superior effort in the great bureaucratic enterprise only by the prospect of unlimited reward is, to say the least, exotic. The contribution to "material progress" of great wealth received by inheritance is, to say even less than the least, a problem. A yet greater problem is the enormous accretions of wealth during the 1980s that were associated, as elsewhere told,[10] with corporate raiding, leveraged buyouts, the related junk-bond promotions, and going on to the impressive rewards received by youthful and industrially quite innocent Wall Street traders, the arbitrage operations of Mr. Ivan Boesky and the junk-bond promotions of Mr. Michael Milken. In the 1980s, the percentage

7. Ibid.
8. Gilder, p. 188.
9. Gilder, p. 118.
10. In Chapter 5.

of very rich Americans — the Forbes Four Hundred — who derived their wealth from financial operations grew enormously. The share gaining great rewards from manufacturing — that is, from clear material progress — declined precipitately.

None of this should be taken as undue criticism; it was Mr. Gilder's achievement, as he himself so generously conceded, to serve not rationality but faith. He saw a demand and filled it, and this he did with literary competence. He made socially serviceable in the strongest terms the uninhibited accumulation of wealth that was essential for the age of contentment. This was the faith he ably affirmed.

Mr. Gilder's faith was supported by numerous advocates, the most articulate, relentless and effective being a former *Wall Street Journal* editorial writer, Jude Wanniski. Mr. Wanniski, in turn, had earlier given a strong endorsement to the taxation doctrine of Professor Arthur Laffer, which was also of notable service to the culture of contentment.

Nothing could more contribute to this culture than a reduction in the share of income its members had to pay in taxes. But here there was a problem. Reducing taxes on the very affluent would mean a reduction in public revenues as a whole. This, in turn, might lead to an increased levy on the middle class or on the tax-paying public in general. Or, by increasing the public deficit, it might have a politically adverse aspect of irresponsibility.

Professor Laffer's contribution was to hold that with such a reduction in taxes, aggregate government revenues would not diminish but increase. This was an especially valuable example of the role of justifying doctrine, however removed from fact.

Proceeding from the undoubted circumstance that if no taxes are levied, no revenue will be collected, and that if taxes absorb all revenue, no income will be produced, Professor Laffer united the two undoubted truths with a freehand curve that showed that with increasing tax rates, aggregate revenues will first rise and then fall. The curve, it has been averred, was originally inscribed rather inexpensively on a paper napkin, perhaps a Kleenex, during dinner in a Washington restaurant.

In a further exercise of imagination, Professor Laffer then held that taxation in the United States had passed the optimal freehand peak. Accordingly, a reduction in taxes would raise total revenues. This then became the case for tax reduction in the age of contentment, and especially in the higher marginal rates on the very affluent.

It is not clear that anyone of sober mentality took Professor Laffer's curve and conclusions seriously. He must have credit, nonetheless, for showing that justifying contrivance, however transparent, could be of high practical service. The tax reduction in the 1980s was, in no slight measure, the product of the Laffer construct. Professor Laffer was not without criticism from professional colleagues, but this in no way detracts from the able service he rendered his constituency.[11]

The statistics are decisive. The average after-tax annual income of those in the upper 20 percent of the income distribution increased in constant dollars from $73,700 in 1981 to $92,000 in 1990.[12] As earlier noted, the income of the average manufacturing worker declined in those same years.

With personal enrichment socially sanctioned and painful progressive taxation mitigated, there still remained the problem of the poor. Their claims, if heard, could result in a continued and costly role for the state. They could seem to justify some reallocation of income from the rich and the comfortable to the impoverished. Here too an appropriate doctrine was required.

And in the mid-1980s, one can now say predictably, the requisite doctrine became available. In a book that went

11. Later history, however, has not been entirely kind to him. A professor at the University of Southern California, he subsequently sought the Republican nomination for one of the United States Senate seats from his home state but gained only slight support. Later still, he found himself in unfortunate if innocent association with a rather well publicized enterprise of seriously questionable character. It appears that Professor Laffer was himself subject to the optimistic financial illusion he so ably exploited in others.

12. Testimony of Robert S. McNamara, former president of the World Bank, before the Budget Committee of the United States House of Representatives, July 30, 1991.

substantially beyond the Laffer Curve in argument and empirical support,[13] Dr. Charles A. Murray provided the nearly perfect prescription. Although the Murray case was stated in rather more elaborate terms, its essence was that the poor are impoverished and are kept in poverty by the public measures, particularly the welfare payments, that are meant to rescue them from their plight. The help becomes a substitute for the personal initiative and effort that would bring true escape.

Dr. Murray's conceptual starting point for remedying the problem would consist of "scrapping the entire federal welfare and income-support structure for working-aged persons, including AFDC (Aid to Families with Dependent Children), Medicaid, Food Stamps, Unemployment Insurance, Worker's Compensation, subsidized housing, disability insurance, and the rest."[14] This, however, he conceded, might, in practice, be extreme. Although, he notes, "[a] large majority of the population [would be] unaffected,"[15] the suffering for some would unquestionably be severe. Accordingly, in a compassionate mood he would keep unemployment compensation. And state and local help and neighborly support and charity would be encouraged for those unable to work and help themselves. But the basic purpose of his argument would be served. The poor would be off the conscience of the comfortable

---

13. *Losing Ground: American Social Policy, 1950–1980* (New York: Basic Books, 1984).

14. Murray, pp. 227–28.

15. Murray, p. 228.

and, a point of even greater importance, off the federal budget and tax system. Dr. Murray's case was argued at no slight length, but the essentials of his very serviceable contribution are here. Nor are the hard facts with which he was dealing in doubt. The number of Americans living below the poverty line increased by 28 percent in just ten years, from 24.5 million in 1978 to 32 million in 1988. By then, nearly one in every five children was born in poverty in the United States, more than twice as high a proportion as in Canada or Germany.[16]

With the Murray formulation the doctrinal basis of the age of contentment was complete: needed encouragement for the rich, lower income taxes with no loss of revenue, reduced spending on the poor and the intellectually impeccable support of Adam Smith. Grouped together, these doctrines made up what was known as "supply-side economics." So far as it had specific content, this meant that economic policy would henceforth be focused not on the factors affecting the flow of aggregate demand in the economy but on those that, by rewarding initiative and therewith production, expanded the economy by increasing the supply of goods and services. To this end, the rich needed the spur of more money, the poor the spur of their own poverty.

In a disturbing interview published in late 1981,[17]

16. McNamara testimony, already cited.
17. With William Greider, "Education of David Stockman," *The Atlantic*, December 1981.

Mr. David Stockman, the Director of the Office of Management and Budget and by far the most visible economic figure in the first Reagan administration, said that the newly espoused doctrines were simply a serviceable cover story; the actual and deeper purpose was to lower taxes on the affluent. Relevant only was the already mentioned trickle-down theory — the less than elegant metaphor that if one feeds the horse enough oats, some will pass through to the road for the sparrows. The forthright nature of the interview provoked a certain stir: members of the new administration were disturbed by the candor; some critics seized happily on the admission; and Mr. Stockman was said, although it was later denied, to have been taken to task rather severely by his President.

The whole episode had, in fact, little consequence. The purpose of the economic ideas identified in this chapter and by Mr. Stockman was to grace the desired action; to the latter they were subordinate. Their service to contentment had its own quite unambiguous force.

9

The Foreign Policy
of Contentment

THE RECREATIONAL
AND THE REAL

BEFORE EXAMINING the way contentment has affected the foreign policy of the United States, it is
important to have in mind certain basic and, indeed, unique features of this area of public policy and
action. These now go seriously unrecognized. This chapter, accordingly, must first depart briefly from the broad
influence of the culture of contentment to place foreign
policy in its public context.

In general, performance in the field of foreign policy,
great emergencies apart, is relatively free from the economic, political and even intellectual requirements and
constraints that control much domestic government action. The latter, because of its effect on taxes, public services and regulation, produces a marked public and
political response, while most foreign policy initiatives,

in contrast, evoke no such reaction. A change in official attitude toward some foreign country, although it may make headlines and the television evening news, does not impinge upon the life of the average citizen. If some peculiarly repressive or abhorrent government is being treated with inappropriate courtesy and grace, there may be objection, even indignation; nonetheless, few Americans are immediately affected in any concrete fashion. Such public response as is heard has the comforting virtue of being rhetorical rather than real, and the adverse opinion can be easily tolerated.

When thoughtful commentators and the press report a deterioration in relations between the United States and some other country, the change has occurred, in practice, only in the attitudes of a limited number of officials on each side. There is no larger involvement or consequence. A newspaper headline saying that the United States government views with grave concern some development in Guatemala, the Philippines or the Ivory Coast means only that a handful of government functionaries have so reacted. Reporting their concern, they *are* the United States. The further consequences of the development are normally slight, as also when, at some later moment, it is said that relations have improved.

The politically and intellectually undemanding character of the routine conduct of foreign affairs is made strongly evident by the way the presumptively responsible personnel come into office. With each new administration high officials of the Department of State are installed, often with no apparent earlier preparation and frequently with no visible qualification.

The even more compelling case is that of so-called political ambassadors assigned to foreign posts. They take command with no prior diplomatic experience of any kind and normally with no prior knowledge of the country to which they are assigned, the name of the capital, in favoring circumstances, possibly apart. Although the practice is subject to occasional criticism, no great damage has been known to result.

The second and closely related feature of foreign policy is the peculiar reward that it accords its practitioners. Those in the government whose responsibility is for domestic policy and administration do, of course, enjoy a certain measure of distinction that comes from identification with the prestige and power of the great Republic; it is for this that so many so reliably seek office. But there is the ever present dark side in the negative reaction from that part of the citizenry that considers their official actions in some way adverse. Contracts and other emoluments have been denied, regulations have been enforced and, on occasion, taxes have been urged, or, at a minimum, there has been association with the expenditure of money that has been reluctantly provided. All of this involves controversy and criticism.

Involvement with foreign policy, on the other hand, is without this unhappy aspect. Instead those thus employed are the actual, visible image of the United States; they bask appreciatively, enjoyably, in its glow.

Men and the few women who have headed missions abroad often seek to retain the ambassadorial title and something of the aforementioned glow for a lifetime. To this end, they attend meetings to hear undemanding accounts of recent developments in foreign policy and often improbable forecasts as to the prospect and to express or reflect on the currently conventional and acceptable views. This latter is in keeping with a larger tendency in foreign policy advice and discussion. Called upon by the President during the Vietnam war, the acknowledged deans of the foreign policy establishment — the Wise Men, as popularly denoted — urged the full, energetic commitment of the armed forces up until the moment when this became palpably disastrous both politically and militarily. Then they advised detachment.

Most revealing, perhaps, as to the recreational character of much modern foreign policy is what happens on the visit to some friendly foreign capital of a President, Vice President or Secretary of State, and the return visit by the foreign leader to the United States. In each case, there is a welcoming ceremony and applause that could not reasonably be expected at home. There follow conversations of quiet, decorous tone, which, however vacuous, are in agreeable contrast with the contentiousness so often experienced in domestic political negotiations. Communiqués are issued, often written in advance, telling imaginatively of the topics under discussion and the areas of agreement.[1] It is believed (and faithfully reported) that in pursuit of foreign policy concerns, high officials travel for important national purpose; not exceptionally, it is, instead, for personal pleasure.

American wealth, economic well-being and the resulting largesse that the United States has distributed overseas have also added in past times to the enjoyments of more substantive foreign policy. American officials and initiatives have received the deference and approving response abroad that in private, public or international relationships accrue to a creditor or to the source of much needed and much welcomed financial endowment. As a result of the Marshall Plan following the Second World War, the ensuing widely dispersed AID programs and the large bank loans to Latin America and other poorer lands, the United States gained the aspect of a rich and generous relative, one to be much respected and warmly thanked. Those who were associated, however marginally, even rhetorically, with those specific programs or with the policy in general delighted in the resulting approval.

From the foregoing it will be evident that foreign policy has a favored role in the polity. It is, to repeat, exempt

---

1. I am aided in my understanding of this process by the fact that I have drafted some of these documents myself. As I have previously observed, no doubt with some exaggeration, it was from this experience that I became aware of my subsequently not unrewarded talent for fiction.

from the harsh attitudes that surround much domestic policy; its conduct and those involved therewith are well regarded. Nor is this a recent development. It far anticipates the mood of the 1980s and President Bush's enthusiastic but wholly natural preference for foreign policy as opposed to socially urgent domestic questions.

The broadly recreational character of foreign policy and its appeal to the community of contentment goes back, in fact, many generations. In the years prior to World War II, a gentleman of financial means derived from inheritance or a monetarily well endowed wife and with a degree from Princeton University, Harvard or Yale could not work for the Department of Agriculture, the Department of Commerce or, certainly, the Department of Labor. But he could serve, with mannered excellence, in the Department of State or in an overseas embassy. The Department had, as has indeed been said, many of the characteristics of an exclusive men's club. Assignment even to countries with the most retrograde governments or dictators could be accepted, even enjoyed, which often resulted in an unfortunate tolerance toward their policies and political activities. In a memorable comment in the early days of the Second World War, President Roosevelt was quoted as saying that the best that could be hoped for from the State Department in the emerging conflict was neutrality.

After the First World War and the Versailles Conference, those diplomats who returned to private life sought diligently to retain the distinction of their recent, greatly prestigious preoccupations and decisions; they formed the Council on Foreign Relations in New York, which, not surprisingly, soon also came to resemble a carefully maintained club. Membership was, as it remains, confined to individuals claiming past experience in foreign policy or, at a minimum, having some academic or journalistic connection therewith. Meetings, although made impressive by an overtone of public concern and responsibility, were held for the undoubted enjoyment of the participants. As might be imagined from the already described nature of foreign policy, the subjects discussed did not normally touch on intellectually challenging, oratorically contentious or politically divisive issues, as would discussions of domestic policy. None had a visible impact on the pay, pocketbooks, profits or the liberties and well-being of the ordinary citizen. Speeches and discussion that were, by well-established custom, kept agreeably within the limits of the accepted wisdom went far to ensure the amiability and calm of the proceedings.[2] The tradition thus so comfortably observed and enjoyed continues and is perpetuated in similarly ceremonial gatherings in other cities and, if in slightly less disciplined fashion, by numerous foreign policy communicants in colleges and universities.

Nor is this enjoyment confined within the geographical

2. I speak as a onetime member of the Council. I have further developed these views in "Staying Awake at the Council on Foreign Relations," *The Washington Monthly* (September 1984), a review of Robert D. Schulzinger, *The Wise Men of Foreign Affairs* (New York: Columbia University Press, 1984).

limits of the United States. In regularly scheduled conferences — those of the Bilderberg convocation and the Trilateral Commission — foreign policy authorities, including past government officials, come pleasurably together for extended discussions not unmixed with mutual admiration. Nothing, or not much, is believed to have emerged from these meetings; they too reflect the recreational aspect of foreign policy in perhaps its highest and most distinguished manifestation.

As compared with the discussion of budgets, taxes, law enforcement, drug abuse, health care or abortion rights, foreign policy is, to repeat, an area of pleasant and relaxing discourse. Anything suggesting political partisanship is regretted and may even be openly deplored. Foreign policy should be "above politics." A good foreign policy for the foreign policy constituency is sternly nonpartisan.

In the United States, as in other countries, and especially in otherwise quiet times, there are certain issues, sometimes ones stirring considerable controversy, such as the American debates over flag burning and the pledge of allegiance and other purely oral patriotic observances in the public schools, that are pursued not because of their intrinsic importance but because the discussion, disagreement and, on occasion, violent collision are greatly enjoyed. At a mild and pleasant level this enjoyment has been extensively true of much foreign policy debate over the years.

*

While no one need regret the polite ceremony and civilized communication that have characterized the past practice of foreign policy, the reality has been at a deeper level. It is possible that amiable and sometimes inspired persuasion has occasionally had useful results, but nearly all foreign policy achievement in the United States has rested on two (and only two) stalwart pillars. These are economic power, with the associated deployment of economic resources, and military power and the threat or actuality of its use. The more purely recreational or rhetorical activities of the foreign policy community count for little in terms of actual change or effect.

American economic strength was the highly visible support to American international influence in the years following the Second World War. The Marshall Plan and the AID programs earlier mentioned, the later American influence in the World Bank and the International Monetary Fund, the compelling need for other countries to gain access to the American market, the perception of the United States as the obvious model of economic success for the world and the extensive resources its private lenders so confidently dispersed with however disastrous consequences were all central to the success of American foreign policy initiatives.

American military power was the second pillar of the American position. These, economic and military strength, were for many years the real as distinct from the rhetorical or recreational basis of American foreign policy. In the age of contentment, however, there has been a marked change in the relative power and importance of the two.

In the decade of the 1980s, as has already been observed, the United States went from being the world's greatest creditor nation to being its greatest debtor. This was of monumental importance to the practice of foreign policy. A creditor has much at his command in the way of proffered support and largesse and commands much respect; a debtor is, alas, reduced to requesting tolerance and assistance for himself. The difference is very great.[3]

Back of the changed economic position of the United States in the world were forces intimately associated with the mood of contentment. The United States and Britain, as also Canada and Australia, emerged in triumph from the Second World War. They, but especially the United States, could look with satisfaction on their wartime military achievements, and they did. From this came the long-lasting mood of self-approval; one does not improve on total success.

The mood in the erstwhile enemy countries, Japan, Ger-

---

3. The economic change that has occurred is not readily conceded. Thus, in *Bound to Lead: The Changing Nature of American Power* (New York: Basic Books, 1990), my distinguished Harvard colleague Joseph S. Nye observes that "the United States remains the largest and richest power with the greatest capacity to shape the future." However, he concedes that there is "an unwillingness [on the part of Americans] to invest in order to maintain confidence in their capacity for international leadership," adding, perhaps resignedly, "in a democracy, the choices are the people's" (p. 261).

many and Italy, was strikingly different. Their history was of unquestioned military disaster, and from this came a sense of needed self-examination, needed improvement and needed effort. On the one hand, the contentment of the victor; on the other, the aspiration of the vanquished.

There is no quantitative measurement that establishes the economic effect of contentment versus aspiration. It is one of the many things in economics and related social comment that depend on the always fragile judgment of the speaker or writer. There were, however, specific, indeed wholly concrete, policies flowing from the difference between defeat and victory.

The defeated countries were left with a powerful sense of the disaster associated with military ambition and with an equally strong awareness of the value of economic excellence, if not superiority. The United States, in contrast, retained a strong commitment to military strength, made stronger, as will be noted presently, by the independent, self-enhancing power of a large military establishment. As a practical consequence, the United States in the 1980s devoted 5.2–6.5 percent of its gross national product to military uses; Germany devoted less than half that; Japan, less than 1 percent.

The American resources so used were at cost to civilian investment and consumption; those so saved in Japan and Germany were available for civilian use and specifically for improving civilian industry. The matter of the use of trained manpower was particularly important. By some calculations, from a quarter to a third of all American scientific and engineering talent in recent years was employed in relatively sterile weapons research and development. This talent the Japanese and the Germans devoted to the improvement of their civilian production. Japan, defeated in war by American industrial power, has now in peacetime extensively replaced its erstwhile enemy in productive service to the American consumer.

And there is more. The United States, with the large overseas debt that has accrued because of the economic policies of the age of contentment, has sharply restrained any foreign policy action that would increase that debt. This is directly the case as to budget expenditure for economic assistance intended to buy foreign economic support or action. Back of this constraint is the haunting specter of higher taxes, the greatest of threats to the controlling principles of contentment.

In the Persian Gulf war of 1991, both Japan and Germany, consistent with their commitment to the superior role of economic power, denied themselves any active military role; in keeping with their perception of economics as the basis of their world position, they offered economic support, support for which the United States with its contrasting emphasis on military strength was reduced to pleading. It did not go wholly unmentioned that the American soldiers, airmen and sailors who led and dominated in the conflict made up what would anciently have been called a mercenary force that was extensively subsidized by Japan, Germany and Saudi Arabia. Nothing so illustrated and emphasized the changed role of economic and military power in American foreign policy as the financial pleas from Washington, the political speeches requesting or demanding more economic support from the allies for military operations.

Other very practical consequences of the decline in American economic power are for all to see. After 1989, as the Eastern European countries and the Soviet Union were seeking the perilous path from socialist and command economies to the market and therewith to a more democratic governing structure, it was vital that this transition be eased with economic help from abroad. It was important that personal liberty and democracy not be identified with empty shops and economic hardship. Such help was forthcoming from the West only reluctantly, and most reluctantly from the United States. Generous offers were made of economic advice, a singularly uncostly contribution.

In the age of contentment, as noted, much foreign policy was passive and recreational in nature, its two principal and substantial supports being economic and military power. As we have seen, only military power has now escaped unimpaired, and with it the next two chapters are concerned.

10

The Military Nexus, I

IN ONE of his earliest and most frequently quoted observations upon becoming President, Ronald Reagan said that in the United States, government was not the solution to problems, it was the problem. Thereafter he made one exception: speaking of government workers, he averred that only those in the armed forces or in support thereof were truly essential.

In defining a political attitude, truth may well emerge from hyperbole; the President was again at one with his constituency. In the years of contentment there were, in fact, and as we have seen, numerous government functions that were indispensable for sustaining the mood of the voting majority. It would have been politically fatal to attack Social Security, old-age pensions, in any comprehensive way. Or publicly supported health care; accident or illness is an expensive and worrisome contingency even for the well rewarded. Support to farm income was equally favored, as was government rescue of failing financial institutions and therewith those who have entrusted their money thereto. Individuals with insured bank accounts ranging up to $100,000 have, generally speaking, more money than those who do not. If a bank is very large — too large to fail — even, or perhaps especially, the largest depositors are rescued. Socialism is deeply abhorrent in the culture of contentment but not for the financially most contented.

In summary, government may be the problem for contentment but not when well-being is in jeopardy. Even President Reagan, were he given to reflection, would have ascribed a necessary function to that which serves or sustains well-being, or, perhaps more precisely, he would have been led to do so by his advisers and staff. Adverse action here would have placed his supporters immediately and visibly at risk, and they would have become vocal in their criticism. However, in defense of Mr. Reagan it must be said that the exception he accorded the military was politically perceptive. The attitudes and interests of his constituency on this subject were especially strong and clear. And so they remain. With economic power, military power is, as we have already seen, one of the two effective pillars of foreign policy — the real as distinct from the rhetorical.

During the past half century less a few years, the most significant support to the deeply embedded position of the military establishment in the culture of contentment was the perception that it was a bulwark against Communism, this being, as noted, the most obtrusive of the seeming threats to contentment. Fear of this was deep and fundamental in the psyche of the contented. Imperiled freedom, loss of liberty, was much cited; especially acute was the threat to private property. Yet earlier, in the period immediately following the First World War, as again in the latter 1940s and the 1950s, the fear of domestic Communism assumed paranoiac proportions. The Palmer raids to round up, imprison and expel presumed foreign subversives were the earlier response; McCarthyism became the code word for the second episode. For anything so enjoyed as the life of the contented there must, as a psychological necessity, be a threatening counterforce. To enjoy life without envisaging such a possibility is seen as a careless evasion of hard reality. And there was the highest level of affirmation: Marxist scholarship over a century and more had identified the greatly privileged — the comfortable owners of property — as the Communists' natural target. That the very majority now enjoying comfort had totally changed the situation — that there were now not a few self-regarding and exploitative capitalists but a mass of superbly satisfied successors — went largely unnoticed. After Palmer, J. Edgar Hoover and McCarthy, the true situation came to be realized in retrospect. Paranoia was seen to be paranoia. The threat of a Communist takeover at home — of "a conspiracy so immense"[1] — was seen to be ridiculous, even mentally aberrant.

1. The sardonic title of a book by David M. Oshinsky (New York: Free Press, 1983).

Nonetheless, Communism remained a compelling cause of fear, undiminished as an international menace even as the domestic alarm subsided and became mildly absurd. Some of this concern was, as with foreign policy, recreational in character. Those presuming to experience, knowledge and authority in such matters gathered with much pleasure and no operational purpose to discuss and to agree on "the threat of Communism" in the world at large; it was not necessary that anything new or distracting be articulated. The major threat was, of course, posed by the Soviet Union and its Eastern European satellites. But were we to be safe, we must resist Communism wherever it appeared in the world. This included those primitive societies that had yet to experience capitalism, even though on the authority of Marx, no less, Communism before capitalism was held to be premature and wholly implausible.

From this anxiety came the greatest of all exceptions to the general constraint on public expenditure. No politician, regardless of formal party identification, could have it said that he or she was "soft on Communism." Given the need to avoid such calumny and aware that military power was central to an effective resistance, he or she could not safely vote against appropriations for the military establishment or its weaponry. That, in turn, was to be "soft on defense."

The fear of Communism was also responsible for three major developments in the military power as that existed in the political economy of contentment. The first, supplementing and extending what was an already large expenditure, was a further enormous increase in military and defense spending as the constituency of contentment gained full power in the 1980s; this was the Reagan arms buildup. The second was the emergence of a largely autonomous military establishment standing above and apart from democratic control. The third was a series of foreign ventures designed ostensibly to arrest the threatening spread of Communism but with the further purpose of justifying the expanding role of the military establishment by providing a presumed enemy. The last two of these developments will be considered in the chapter that follows.

The most common of all public references to government activities in the United States during the decade of the 1980s was to the defense buildup. Expenditures in the decade increased from $143 billion in 1980 to $314 billion in 1990, in constant 1990 dollars from $206 billion to $314 billion.[2] This was not in response to any new military threat; that was not even suggested. It was fully in response to the fears of the constituency of contentment that was now solidly in power.

There was, indeed, broad recognition that the nuclear arsenal being so enlarged reflected a vast, indeed numer-

2. *Economic Report of the President*, February 1991.

ically incredible, potential overkill. And it was known that no small part of the buildup was based on symbolism, not reality. Aged and stately battleships, many years from the shipyard, were dug out of mothballs and refurbished at considerable cost, although it was accepted that in any war of serious consequence their vulnerability would be extreme. The Strategic Defense Initiative, or SDI, commonly called Star Wars, went forward in the face of the all but universally held view of competent engineers and scientists that there was no rational reason to suppose that it would work. Such at its extreme fringes was the legacy of the fear of Communism. However, present also, as earlier indicated, were very tangible financial rewards. Expenditures for defense, like the bailing out of the banks and the savings and loan associations and unlike welfare or educational spending in the central cities, rewarded individuals — executives, scientists, engineers, political lobbyists, many weapons industry workers — who were solidly in the larger constituency of contentment.

Before going on to further consideration of the role of the military in the culture of contentment, it is necessary, however, to consider the most seriously discommoding feature of the commitment to the military, one that has been handled with no slight intelligence and even subtlety in recent years. This is the grave inconvenience for the community of contentment of personal service in the armed forces by oneself or by one's offspring, with the further possibility of participation in combat and the associated threat of dismemberment or highly premature death. In the part of the world where life has little to offer, this is not a matter of equal relevance. It is one of the reasons, perhaps the prime reason, that armed conflict and death are so extensively the fate of the poorest people on the planet. Not remarkably, they are the most easily persuaded that the next life will be better because for many it could not be worse. To the contented, obviously, this situation does not apply. Service in the armed forces and the implied threat of actual warfare and all its dangers are therefore to be avoided. So it was in the United States in the age of contentment.

In the years of the Vietnam war, North Vietnam was, in any serious American view, remote and improbable as a Communist threat. Nonetheless, there was substantial support for the war from the then nascent community of contentment. This, however, did not extend to those with sons of military age, and notably it did not to the sons themselves, vulnerable as they were to recruitment. The universities, the prime locus of the relatively affluent young, became the center of resistance to the war and very specifically to the draft. This resistance, as the years passed and the hostilities continued, became formidable and, as regards the continued prosecution of the war, decisive. There was no similar adverse reaction from poorer youths or those of the underclass.

The obvious and, indeed, inevitable step in response was taken in 1973 with the suspension of general military conscription. It was accepted that the contented should not be forced into military service. This, with its attendant discomforts and dangers, would be reserved for those who could be attracted from less agreeable surroundings by pay, training and the general prospect for economic betterment. These promises became the theme of armed forces recruiting and were made widely familiar through television advertising, which abandoned patriotism as a plea and promised instead immediate economic advantage and subsequent advance. The anciently most unacceptable feature of the military nexus — the distinctly adverse thought and possibility of death in combat — was thus shifted from the contented to the aspiring members of the underclass and, in larger measure, to those verging thereon. This the social and economic composition of the armed forces in the age of contentment fully affirmed, although no slight effort was made to interpret the figures in the best possible way.

Thus, a survey of recruits to active service in 1987 that was based on the income of the communities whence they came[3] showed markedly fewer from the age-eligible pop-

3. Richard L. Fernandez, *Social Representation in the U.S. Military* (Congress of the United States: A Study of the Congressional Budget Office, October 1989), pp. 40–41. The communities were the postal ZIP-code districts for which family income figures were available from the 1980 census.

ulation as incomes passed the $19,600–$23,300 range.[4] The number fell steadily as average incomes increased; the fewest recruits were from the highest-income communities, and they, quite possibly, were from the poorer families therein.

The youth from the higher-income areas, to the extent that they served at all, also showed an intelligent preference, aided by better education, for the Navy and Air Force, as opposed to the less pleasant and personally less safe prospect of service with the ground forces.

Seeking rather ostentatiously to put the best face on this troubling matter, the above-cited study observed that "high-income areas may be underrepresented among recruits, but they are not *un*represented. Of the 100 wealthiest ZIP-code areas, all with median family incomes exceeding $40,000 in 1979, fewer than one-quarter did not provide a single male recruit in 1987. . . . The roster of areas represented [by recruits] includes the Los Angeles suburbs of Bel Air and Beverly Hills, California, and the Chicago suburbs of Kenilworth, Glencoe and Winnetka, Illinois."[5] It will be thought that a representation of only one, two or a handful from an affluent community does not deny the more general escape from this unwelcome obligation. The author of the study in question is him-

4. These were 1979 income levels as shown by the 1980 census and are expressed in 1979 dollars. See Fernandez, p. 40.
5. Fernandez, pp. 42–43.

self impelled to note that there are anecdotal poor in even the wealthiest community.

That minorities are overrepresented in the armed forces is, of course, conceded. In 1989 blacks accounted for approximately 22 percent of active-duty recruits, as compared with 14 percent of all enlistment-age youth. In the Army — the service that is, as noted, the most threatened by uncomfortable service and death in battle — the proportion was above 25 percent.[6] That in the age of contentment the marked inconveniences and dangers anciently associated with military service were substantially shifted to those outside the favored community is evident.

Support to the military with its reward to those who supply it with weaponry and its discriminate call for military service is, it will be reasonably clear, in keeping with the interests of the community of contentment. But the latter is not its only source of power. There is grave error in thinking the military is accountable only to broad polit-

6. In January 1991, before the outbreak of the war in the Persian Gulf, Congressman Les Aspin, Chairman of the Armed Services Committee of the United States House of Representatives, scheduled hearings on the socioeconomic composition of the forces at risk in Saudi Arabia. Having looked into this matter, I was invited to testify. As war became imminent and then arrived, the hearings, twice scheduled, were first postponed and then canceled. The issue, it seems possible, was thought too delicate for extended (and possibly adverse) public exploration at that time. With actual hostilities at hand, the favored position of the contented could not be too blatantly discussed.

ical and democratic decisions; under the protective cloak of democracy it is also strongly self-sustaining. This is a matter of prime importance. Nor is it a situation peculiar to the United States. In many countries, and especially in the Third World, as it is called, the military enjoys a position of independent power, and it is this that will be discussed in the next chapter.

11

The Military Nexus, II

THAT THE MILITARY ESTABLISHMENT has enjoyed exemption from the more general constraint on public action and public expenditure during the age of contentment has been sufficiently stressed. It is not seriously in doubt, nor, perhaps, is the substantial support it received in the past from the fear of Communism. This, however, explains only part of the present role and power of the military. There is also what may be called the autonomous power of great organization, a power that acts with particular force in the case of the military establishment. And there is the more than convenient tendency for formal and conventional thought and theory to conceal the true character and even the existence of this autonomous or internally generated power.

We have seen its elements — and its concealment — in the organizations of ordinary civilian economic life, and here I must refer back to matters earlier discussed. The great business enterprise, it is assumed and taught, is in the service of the consumer and is subject in all important respects to his or her sovereign authority. This service is said to be solely in pursuit of profit maximization. There can be monopoly or otherwise imperfect competition that allows the firm to extract undue compensation for what it does for the consumer; there can also be, although, as earlier noted, this is rarely discussed, bureaucratic incompetence. These are aberrations. The consumer remains in command. This the tens of thousands who are subject to scholarly economics instruction are taught every year.

In fact, the consumer is very substantially in the service of the business firm. It is to this end that advertising and merchandising in all their cost and diversity are directed; consumer wants are shaped to the purposes and notably to the financial interests of the firm. This is not a subtle exercise of power; television advertising, a more than slightly ostentatious instrument of persuasion, is not easily overlooked.

Nor is profit maximization, the presumptively controlling motivation in market response, uniformly operative. Management in the large organization may instead be concerned primarily with its own security, prerogatives, perquisites and power, and with defending these against intruders — a deeply destructive phenomenon, as has also already been noted. And members of the organization may have a general commitment to bureaucratic stability and comfort. Such are the frequent, wholly visible tendencies of great organization.

They are not, however, visible in conventional economic teaching and more general discourse. Here the market is a semireligious totem; in the market economy, instruction as to wants and needs proceeds ineluctably from consumer to producer. That the former is in some measure the instrument of the latter, that the great producing firm serves not a public purpose but its own, is thus removed from sight and thought. In much formal economic discussion extending on into the textbooks there is a measure of discontent and sometimes impatience when these matters are pressed. The market has its own truth on which reality does not intrude. We see here how effectively, even brilliantly, the preferred ideas can subsume and control inconvenient reality where organization is concerned.

The self-contained power that is thus exercised in civilian life is, however, of rather small importance and effect as compared with its much greater manifestation in the military establishment. On any detached examination, the latter — the armed services, the associated and supporting bureaucracy and the supplying business enterprises, principally the weapons firms — has a power, certainly has had a power, far transcending that of any civilian organization, certainly of any private business firm.

In all economic life there are two primary constraints on organization power. One is external authority over what is produced — in civilian life the ultimate decision of the consumer, however influenced by advertising and other persuasion. The other is the flow of purchasing power —

in economic terms, the effective demand — that is available for the purchase of the good or service. The special, even unique character of the military establishment is that neither of these constraints is operational; both authority over what is produced and effective demand are, or have been, substantially within the control of the military establishment itself. The military forces and facilities that are to be maintained are extensively a military decision; the weapons to be developed and produced, and therewith the money to procure them, are also all but exclusively a military decision.

An important ceremonial role is played by the civilian heads of the defense establishment; it has long been recognized that with the rarest, most eccentric exceptions, they are effectively the captives of the establishment as a whole, or, as the case may be, the Army, Air Force or Navy department that is nominally their responsibility. It is indicative of this power, or more exactly of its absence, that the names of these civilians in the several services, the departmental secretaries, are no longer known even in Washington. That one of them should stand in strong opposition to the interest of the service he heads is nearly unthinkable. Tenure in these positions is also brief, and, in the nearly normal case, the occupant and also his civilian subordinates move on to jobs in the defense industry — either direct employment or remunerative service as consultants. In effect, all are part of the complex itself, of a closed circle of common interest — a point that, indeed, is now widely accepted.

There is also, it will be observed, the role of the Congress and its committees. This too has long been partly ceremonial. The armed services committees attract, as a matter of course, legislators whose interests accord closely with those of the military. All are given careful and rewarding attention by high military officers and civilian officials. Some, through political action committees, are broadly in the pay of the defense firms. Others, as also legislators in general, are held hostage by the defense firms and military installations in their home districts or states. Thus Senator Alan Cranston of California, long a critical voice on the power of the military, found it necessary to make an exception for the B-2 bomber, a prospective source of substantial income and employment in his state. Thomas J. Downey, a vigorous and effective spokesman for arms control from Long Island, New York, was required to speak for the survival of the military aircraft production of the Grumman Corporation in his own congressional district.

Other legislators, similarly pressed, had no similar problem of conscience in coming to the support of their local defense production. And numerous legislators with no commitment either as to conscience or constituency have been no less ardently, even automatically, in the service of the military. As previously observed, a legislator could not be thought soft on Communism, and equally he or she could not be thought soft on defense. The result has been substantial military control of the legislative process, as of the presumptively responsible but extensively ceremonial civilian authority. Thus consolidated are the two vital sources of power. The military establishment largely determines the military mission that it pursues and the manpower and weaponry that support it. And, effectively, it controls the support or funding — the effective demand — for that mission, manpower and weaponry. None may say that this power is total or without occasional impairment; nothing is ever gained by exaggeration. Of this a word presently. That there is, in the nature of great organization, a sharply autonomous power here will not, in any detached view, be doubted.

Another important point is that just as the power of the great corporate enterprise is held to be under the benign constraints of the market, so the military power has long been held to be under the equally benign authority of democracy. What exists is said to be an expression of democratic will. Democracy is here, as elsewhere, the gracing note for a singularly independent and self-reinforced exercise of authority. It is the rood screen, perhaps more precisely the altar, behind which the modern military-industrial complex enjoys its self-generated and self-serving autonomy.

There is, as suggested in the preceding chapter, one further requirement if the military power is to be fully sustained. That is an enemy. This is not a primary need; as we have seen, the military establishment — the great organization that is currently extant — has emanating from within itself a full justification of its role. Nonetheless a visible threat is also important.

During the age of contentment there was no doubt as to the enemy. It was the Soviet Union and its presumed allies, the members of the Warsaw Pact,[1] and the underlying threat of Communism, extending on into the Third World. Here, however, there was difficulty. Preparation for war, the arms race, would admirably serve the military power. A nuclear war, however, would not; it would, the view of suicidal intransigents apart, be destructive of that power, as of all else. In consequence, during the Reagan and early Bush years there was, instead, a succession of small military exercises of no enduring pain or importance. Marines were sent into Lebanon for largely unspecified purposes, although they were quickly withdrawn as they came under severe terrorist attack. Bombers were sent to destroy Muammar Qaddafi in Libya but managed to strike only some unfortunate adjacent bystanders instead. There was a military excursion to Grenada, there to unseat an allegedly dangerous Communist head of government and assure the benign control of an allegedly threatening airport then under construction. There was

---

1. Even though there was doubt, even in the Reagan years, of the full utility of the members of that organization as adversaries. At a meeting in Washington in the 1980s, an informed, more than slightly undisciplined but distinctly amused member of the Pentagon staff observed in private conversation that in the case of war the Hungarian divisions were potentially much more damaging to the Soviets than those of Poland. The Polish divisions, being relatively efficient, would change sides very quickly and thus be out of the way. The Hungarians, militarily incompetent, would stand in place and be a major barrier to effective deployment and operations.

the more serious descent on Panama to arrest a former CIA anti-Communist asset, General Manuel Noriega, who had turned his attention to the drug traffic. Trading on the anti-Communist paranoia, there were slightly more subtle military interventions in Afghanistan, Angola and elsewhere in Africa and Central America, notably in Nicaragua and El Salvador. There was also major arms assistance to the same end in numerous other countries.

That Communism or socialism, a point earlier emphasized, is not a plausible economic and political design in countries that have not experienced capitalism, Angola and Nicaragua being good examples, was not a serious restraining factor. Nor was the evident fact that those countries, as earlier South Vietnam, posed no real security threat to the United States. These matters were raised and dismissed. What was less understood, even by those raising them, was that these objections missed the real point. Such military activities, however remote from any rationally established need, served in an important way the broad purpose of the military establishment. They were visible justification of its eminence and power; small, safe and spectacular, they were a reminder that military force was of continuing relevance. There were limits to which the confrontation with the Soviet Union could be carried, but here there were none. These demonstrations were not, from any seriously offered analysis, in the service of any essential foreign policy advantage; their primary service, as, indeed, was also widely understood, was to the autonomous power of the military establishment.

The point should not be carried to extremes. The need for an enemy and the service of that enemy to the military establishment unquestionably had something, perhaps much, to do with President Bush's decision in January 1991 to intervene in the Middle East against Iraq. That this promised to justify the development of advanced communications and other electronic aircraft and military technology was especially attractive, as was the fact that the troops involved, especially those experiencing the extreme discomforts and casualties of ground combat, did not come from the contented electoral majority. The de facto exemption of the sons and daughters of this class was, without doubt, an important factor in making this particular military venture politically acceptable.[2]

There was, as has indeed been much noted, an even more specific service to the military power. The earlier venture into Vietnam and Cambodia had exposed major shortcomings and rather pronounced incompetence in the military, especially in the conduct of jungle warfare against determined guerrilla forces. Iraq, which was indubitably guilty of aggression and, by American standards, was small in population, insignificant in compar-

---

2. Writing this during the days when the conflict was under way and much applauded, I asked the Harvard dean responsible for student matters how many of his charges had rallied to the war or been commanded thereto. He replied, "Very few." I pressed for a precise figure. He replied, "Zero."

ative industrial power and openly exposed on the desert, was admirably designed to retrieve the military reputation. The war was prosecuted with dispatch and at low cost in American casualties. It was favorably reported because of the impressive and generally successful control over the attendant and often unduly cooperative press. While there were dissonant voices that made reference to the heavy death rate among Iraqi civilians and the visibly reluctant Iraqi soldiers who had been forced into combat, and to the generally unfortunate, even disastrous, political aftermath, there is little doubt that the war in the Gulf did much for the reputation and prestige of the military establishment. In the celebrations marking the return of the victorious soldiers, no opportunity for enhancing this prestige was lost.

The collapse of Communist power in Eastern Europe at the end of the 1980s, the evident upheaval and disassociation within the Soviet Union itself, and the overthrow of the Communist Party there were thought by many to presage a major change in the position, power and control over financial resources of the American military establishment. The term *peace dividend* became part of the language. This underestimated the autonomous character of the military power. The military budget was only mildly affected by these events. The development of weapons systems, now unrelated to a plausible enemy, continued generally as before. Weapons technology was seen to have its own independent and affirming mission. An enemy was useful but not essential.

Yet here a final qualification must, indeed, be entered. The collapse of Communism and the disintegration of the Soviet Union are not small events; they constitute the greatest transformation on the world scene in the last half century and more. The military power may well not escape the consequences, and what the ultimate effect on it will be no one can know. Modest reductions are possible. What is certain, however, is that it will yield neither easily nor completely to change. Exports of weaponry to other countries will be encouraged and financed. Understanding of politics in our time will continue to require an appreciation of the depth and breadth and influence of the modern military power.

12

The Politics of Contentment

IN THE PAST, it is clear, the contented and the self-approving were a small minority in any national entity; left outside were the majority of the citizenry. Now in the United States the favored are numerous, greatly influential of voice and a majority of those who vote. This, and not the division of voters as between political parties, is what defines modern American political behavior. This, and not the much celebrated circumstance of charismatic political leaders and leadership, is what shapes modern politics. The leaders, a point sufficiently emphasized, are a reflection of their supporting constituency. Dominating and omnipresent on television, in the polls and in the press, they are passive or accommodating as to the political reality. Of that they are the product. Less dramatic but not dissimilar is the situation in other industrial countries, a matter on which there will be a later word.

The Republican Party in the United States is the accepted representative of the comfortable and contented, the effective instrument of the economic principles and political behavior patterns hitherto identified therewith. There are, as always, a number of dissonant voices. Some formal dissent has long been heard from within the party as to macroeconomic policy, with budget deficits being specifically subject to grave verbal expressions of alarm. Overwhelmingly, however, the Republican Party accepts the commitment to short-run serenity as opposed to longer-run concern. It stands for a diminished role of government, the already noted exceptions for military expenditure, financial rescue and Social Security apart. Taxation is powerfully resisted; it is accepted that the rich and the relatively affluent need the incentive of good income as, if said more discreetly, the poor are deserving of their poverty. In presidential elections since 1980, the commitment of the Republicans to the policies of contentment has been the source of their marked success — victories by substantial majorities of those voting. Their Democratic opponents have found themselves faced with a seemingly intractable problem, and this they have generally resolved by also aligning themselves with the beliefs and the needs of the contented. Since the Republicans have a longer tradition of and a greater aptitude for satisfying this particular constituency, the Democrats have been defeated.

Many who vote Democratic, perhaps a majority, are, in fact, strongly committed to the politics of contentment. They are Democrats by local or family tradition. In the South and Southeast especially, but elsewhere as well, they combine inherited and regional attitudes with the economics of personal contentment and are openly known as *conservative* Democrats. They would vote Republican were there any threat of serious onslaught on the policies of contentment, and many have, in fact, made the transition. This they would all certainly do, were a Democratic presidential candidate to make a concerted political bid for those not similarly favored — those, as a prime example, who live in the desolation of the large inner cities. No action on behalf of the latter — improved welfare payments, more low-income housing, general health care, better schools, drug rehabilitation — could be taken without added public cost, and from this would come the decisive threat of higher taxation. Accordingly, in a dominant Democratic view, reference to such effort must be downplayed or, as necessary, avoided. It looms large in conversation, small in declared intent. Liberals, as they are known, are especially warned: whatever their personal opinion as to the larger well-being or the longer future, they must be practical. If they want to win, they must not invade the community of contentment. Some, and perhaps a considerable number, would feel obliged to desert a candidate strongly committed to the underclass and those now nonparticipant in the electoral system. The shock effect to comfort would even here be too severe.

There are, of course, other factors that support the politics of contentment. In the United States there is the powerful effect of money on public attitudes and political action, and money, in singular measure, is what the contented majority enjoys and deploys. It is to this audience that television and the press are directed. In consequence, the perception of government as an onerous and unnecessary burden, the presumptively self-inflicted wounds of the poor, even the cover stories emphasizing the high social utility of the returns to the rich, acquire acceptance as the reputable view. Inevitably, the commonly believed becomes the truth. Those who appeal too obviously to the poor are said to be not only politically impractical, they are in conflict with accepted reality. It helps, none can doubt, that those who report and comment on political matters — the representatives of the media — themselves belong to the contented majority, as do those who employ them or provide the income that sustains their employment. To be sure, the public and journalistic ethic requires that this never be admitted; there can, however, be surrender to a subdued but persuasive influence when the influence is unrecognized by those so surrendering.

And there is the more direct effect of money. This, indeed, is much discussed in our time. Elections have become exceedingly expensive, and, in one subtle or less subtle fashion or another, public salaries are supplemented from private sources. The sources of the needed funds are all but invariably the economically comfortable. They must be accorded deference, for it is from them that comes the wherewithal to contest elections as well as, in the frequent case, to sustain an agreeable personal living standard.

*

The political strategy, as rather loosely it is called, of Democratic candidates in recent presidential elections follows from the controlling factors just mentioned. There emerges here the self-styled political expert, even genius, who, being relentlessly available, is celebrated by the unduly susceptible representatives of the media. The amply advertised qualification for such a job is normally some past success in a secondary electoral contest, there being a still unrevealed certainty that he, or somewhat exceptionally she, will now lose the next one. In fact, the principal talent necessary is an accomplished mastery of elementary arithmetic.

From this modest mathematical competence comes the conclusion: to win, one must subtract voters from the other side. Accordingly, a Democratic presidential candidate must be no less acquiescent to the contented majority than the Republican. This requires that he make no serious bow to the nonparticipating, nonvoting minority; that would arrest all recruitment from the opposition with the further chance of losing comfortable Democratic voters.[1] In consequence of the foregoing, all

1. Having been a frequent speechwriter in presidential elections beginning with the Roosevelt campaign in 1940, I have had a close exposure to the above-mentioned arithmetical basis of political strategy and to its use by the current political strategist. As I've often told, he has leaned over my shoulder on the candidate's airplane to watch the words of a speech in progress on my typewriter.
"Professor, you can't say that."
"It's what our man believes, what the people need."
"Look, if you say that, you will alienate those who are already most against us."

recent presidential elections have been fought between twin exponents of the broad position of the contented majority. In 1988 the Democratic candidate, Michael Dukakis, largely abandoning the issues that might be adverse to the culture of contentment, made as his principal claim his "competence." Not surprisingly, the traditional and seemingly more reliable exponent of comfort won. Many decades ago President Harry S. Truman observed in a memorable comment that when there was a choice between true conservatives and those in pragmatic approximation thereto, the voters would always opt for the real thing.

While the foregoing is the broad rule by which American electoral politics should be understood, there are, as in the case of all political matters, exceptions to be noted.

There is, first, the intruding role of international relations, and notably that of armed conflict. The major wars of this century — the two World Wars, the Korean and the war in Vietnam — were fought under Democratic auspices. In all four cases, the immediate instinctive support was strong; with the exception of World War II, the ultimate effect, however, was to bring the political opposition back into office. The public preference, even that of the more ardent supporters of military expenditure, is for short, comfortable, successful and not unduly expensive wars. These, as earlier noted, the Republicans have provided in Grenada, Panama and Iraq. The Democratic fate has been wars of enduring pain, high fiscal cost and, in the case of Korea and Vietnam, with no dramatically successful conclusion.

There is also the somewhat different circumstance that applies to candidates for state and local office and particularly for the Congress. Here for traditional reasons, and largely in the South, it is possible for Democrats to appeal to the comfortable and contented and win election. In the larger cities and in older industrial areas, on the other hand, the Democrats must appeal to the socially concerned and to the discontented or dissatisfied, which in the particular constituency make up an electoral majority. The combination of these three sources of support — the traditional, the socially concerned and the discontented — has enabled the Democrats to maintain a majority in the two houses of Congress, but it has been at the cost of a sharp split between the traditionalists who serve the politics of contentment and those who have constituencies of comparative discontent or who are otherwise susceptible thereto.

Two matters concerning the politics of contentment remain. Those responding to its persuasion are a majority of those voting in the United States; they are not, as we have sufficiently seen, a majority of the adult population. Some who do not vote are illegal aliens; more are recently arrived from less favored lands and are awaiting citizenship. Thus, for some members of the underclass, squalor and privation are not exceptional, and there may be a sense of gratitude from having escaped something worse. However, the larger justification for not voting is that, for the reasons just given, it is an idle exercise for the eligible poverty-ridden citizen. It is rightly perceived that the difference between the two parties on the immediately affecting issues is inconsequential; accordingly, why bother to decide between them? Thus the majority rule of the contented is or has been ensured.

It follows further that presidential and legislative action or, more seriously, inaction, however adverse and alienating the effect on the socially excluded — homelessness, hunger, inadequate education, drug affliction, poverty in general — is under the broad sanction of democracy. A disturbing parallel, one already suggested, emerges here. Prior to the great revolt of 1989–90 in Eastern Europe, dissatisfaction and alienation were under the broad gloss of socialism; if the people had socialism, they could not be unhappy. The case is now similar in language in the United States: this is the democratic system; systemically it is above error. The fact that a full half of the population does not participate in presidential elections, yet fewer in congressional contests, does not go unnoticed, but it also does not impair the assumption that democracy is controlling and benign.

Finally, there is the question of whether, and to what extent, the politics of contentment, which is so evident in the United States, extends to other industrial countries. There can be little doubt that it does. In the United Kingdom a contented majority ensured the rule of the government of Margaret Thatcher for eleven years, even though in the Midlands and to the north unemployment and exclusion were a continuing source of social discontent.

Unlike the Democrats in the United States, however, the British Labour Party, its more extreme and vocal dissidents kept largely under control, has continued to be seen as an alternative to the contented majority. In consequence, its members have still considered elections a worthwhile opportunity, and they have still gone to the polls to vote. They have also gained strength as the more dramatic actions of Mrs. Thatcher's government, most notably the poll tax as a substitute for local property levies (since partly repealed), have discountenanced the less affluent of the contented majority. In consequence, the political position of contentment may now be rather less secure in Britain than in the United States. And perhaps the case is the same in Canada, where a conservative government has by taxation and trade policy[2] somewhat similarly narrowed the political base of contentment.

In Western Europe there has been a different development. There, in Scandinavia, Germany, the Low Countries, Austria, France and Switzerland, strong social legislation has brought most of the citizenry into the contented majority. And accompanying and supporting this development has been the already mentioned large im-

---

2. Specifically, the free trade agreement with the United States, which has resulted in Canada's loss in plant, employment and customers to its southern neighbor.

portation of labor from lower-wage countries to replace those of the contented who have removed themselves from hard, nonprestigious physical toil. With some noteworthy exceptions, these foreign workers do not or cannot vote, but since they are there as an exercise of their own will, they do not complain about being disenfranchised or they are not able to do so. Accordingly, the position of the contented majority in Western Europe, under whatever political label, seems relatively secure.

A final word on politics. As in economics nothing is certain save the certainty that there will be firm prediction by those who do not know. It is possible that in some election, near or far, a presidential candidate will emerge in the United States determined to draw into the campaign those not now impelled to vote. Conceivably those so attracted — those who are not threatened by higher taxes and who are encouraged by the vision of a new governing community committed to the rescue of the cities and the impacted underclass — could outnumber those lost because of the resulting invasion of contentment. If this happens, the effort would succeed.

It will be evident from these pages that that is not a glowing prospect.

So much for the way contentment has affected politics and political theory. Attention must now be turned to its larger consequences.

13

The Reckoning, I

THE PROBLEMS and evidently adverse prospects of the American economy and polity and of the position of the United States in the world have not escaped notice. On the contrary, they have sustained a large literature of varying competence and insight, all of which has one significant feature in common: all expresses faith in change and correction. These will be the natural outcome of an informed public and eventually of a wise and determined leadership. In consequence, any contemplation of the present American position, however depressing, always sees a better future. One does not, should not, doubt the self-corrective capacity of democracy.[1]

The difficulty with this assumption will be evident. We

1. There are exceptions. My alert and perceptive colleague Robert B. Reich observes that "without the support of the fortunate fifth [of the population], it will be almost impossible to muster the resources, and the political will, necessary for change." *The Work of Nations: Preparing Ourselves for 21st-Century Capitalism* (New York: Knopf, 1991), p. 251.

now have democracy — a democracy of the contented and the comfortable. The comfortable monopolize or largely monopolize the political franchise; the uncomfortable and the distressed of the poor urban and rural slums and those who identify with their bad fortune do not have candidates who represent their needs and so they do not vote. As has been emphasized, the democracy of contentment is the policy of the untroubled short run, of the accommodating economic and political thought and of a separate and dominating military power. Its foreign policy, devoid of the financial support that was decisive in the past, is heavily dependent on the military and, in keeping with a well-established tradition, is recreational rather than real.

The ancient call to the doctor to "heal thyself" is notably without effect if the doctor, so far from admitting disability and disease, affirms his own full feeling of health. What then is the future?

The leading prospect for change is of some development inherent in the sustaining structure of contentment, one that would drastically challenge the latter and force a new view of society. Attention in the future, as in the past, will be on leaders and legislatures and on the changes they initiate or should initiate. Reality will be with the events that would destroy the mood of contentment. A similar, though rather more restricted mood in the 1920s — the years of Calvin Coolidge and briefly of Herbert Hoover — was brought to an end by the Great

Depression. Without the Depression there would have been no Franklin D. Roosevelt or New Deal. Without the attack on Pearl Harbor and Hitler's insane declaration of war on the United States, Roosevelt's effort to help — and save — Britain would have been greatly delayed and would quite possibly have been ineffective. Dwight D. Eisenhower did not bring to a close the twenty years of Democratic dominance of American politics; that dominance was ended by the Korean War. Eisenhower's very wise role was simply to promise to stop the conflict and escape the death and stalemate in that faraway country. John F. Kennedy and Lyndon Johnson were not the true source of the great movement to civil rights in the states of the erstwhile Confederacy. It was the result, instead, of the violent and nonviolent explosion from below, which challenged the culture of contentment in the South and led on to the remedial legislation. Neither President, however well intentioned, could have acted in the absence of that revolt. The war in Vietnam was brought to an end not by the enlightened vision of Richard Nixon, Gerald Ford and Secretary of State Henry Kissinger, but because it threatened the comfort of a younger generation, and in particular that of its more affluent members who did not wish to fight. There had been grave concern in the United States about the safety of nuclear power generators long before the accident at Three Mile Island, but the latter, at least for a time, effectively ended further investment therein.

The present age of contentment will come to an end

only when *and if* the adverse developments that it fosters challenge the sense of comfortable well-being. As well as the strong and successful political appeal to the disadvantaged I have already mentioned, there are three other plausible possibilities as to how this will happen. They are: widespread economic disaster, adverse military action that is associated with international misadventure, and eruption of an angry underclass. To these I now turn. The economic prospect is the concern of this chapter; the more violent possibilities are in the next.

It is abundantly clear that the short-run economic policies of contentment, protected by the accommodation of economics to comfort, could bring eventual economic discomfort. In the second half of 1990, the economy of the United States entered upon a severe recession. This spread to her trading partners, notably to Canada but also to Europe and beyond. Some of the difficulty was attributed conveniently, even imaginatively, to the prospect and then the actuality of war in the Persian Gulf. That the primary responsibility lay with the immediately preceding economic policy is not, however, in doubt. The mergers and acquisitions and leveraged buyouts had left corporations with a heavy burden of debt and interest payments, and the more extravagant cases lapsed into bankruptcy. Those that escaped all but automatically cut new investment (including that in research and development) in order to remain solvent. There was a further and implicit brake on business investment and also home building because of the decade-long reliance on monetary policy — the effort by thc Federal Reserve Board to control inflation with high real interest rates. (It is, to repeat, by limiting investment expenditure and borrowing by consumers that monetary policy acts against inflation.) These high interest rates did not, however, restrain extreme speculative activity in commercial and luxury residential building, and when the collapse in that area came, it left the banking system with heavy losses. The solvency of numerous banks was threatened, a good number failed, and lending was curtailed by all. Some large insurance companies were also similarly affected, those that were heavily encumbered with junk bonds and diversely bad loans. Meanwhile the savings and loan larceny and collapse dried up a further source of funds for real estate purchase and development and left a heavy overhang of questionable properties to find a market. The ultimate effect was a deep depression in the construction industry, producing therein nearly total unemployment in some areas. Unemployment in other occupations showed a marked increase as both consumer and investor confidence diminished.

The long years of high budget deficits when they were not needed made it seemingly impossible to initiate stimulating public expenditures when they were now needed. The celebrated tax reductions for the upper-income brackets and the accompanying economies in welfare distribution had substituted the discretionary spending of the rich for the wholly reliable spending of the poor. A reasonably equitable distribution of income is thought by individuals of liberal disposition to be politically virtuous; in fact, it is economically highly functional.

In the years of contentment there had also been a sharp curtailment of central government support to state and local governments. This was plausible: federal aid to these governments exposes their services and the cost of those services to the federal income tax, and protection from that levy is central to the culture of contentment. With the recession, accordingly, the states and localities were faced with the choice of raising their more regressive taxes, cutting services that were meant extensively for the less privileged and the poor, or doing both. All three courses of action, the subject of great and angry debate, were well designed to make the recession both more painful and worse.

A severe recession or depression could, indeed, shake the political economy of contentment and lead to change. This, as just noted, happened during the Great Depression. And there has long been a lurking fear that it was about to happen again. A small cottage industry existed in the 1980s in the manufacture of books detailing the nature and certainty of a forthcoming economic debacle.[2] However, economic prediction regularly outruns the available knowledge, and this could be the case here. A severe

2. The leading practitioner, Dr. Ravi Batra, found a very large audience for his volume *The Great Depression of 1990* (New York: Simon and Schuster, 1987).

depression as the end of the age of contentment is even now far from certain.

There is, first of all, the undoubted fact that many people could sit quietly in comfort in the worst of times. So situated, they would not, at the very least, respond with enthusiasm to the measures that would alleviate economic adversity and its painful effect on others. It is unfortunate that human feeling is not more sensitive, but so it is.

In the 1930s, the community of well-being powerfully resented the ameliorating measures promulgated by Franklin Roosevelt. He came to office in 1932 partly on the strength of a powerful promise to balance the federal budget and otherwise batten down the hatches for the then still comfortable. In this respect, as I have earlier indicated, his election involved a substantial measure of deception, and in ensuing years he was pilloried as no President has been since for his failure to keep the faith; he was widely called a traitor to his class, the class being then smaller but fully as contented. The American Liberty League, a business and financial convocation that identified freedom, as so often, with privileged affluence, came into existence solely to oppose him. Of the Social Security Act of 1935, the most durable and important of the curative actions, a leading congressional spokesman for the opposition said, with no intended exaggeration, "Never in the history of the world has any measure been brought in here so insidiously designed as to prevent business recovery, to enslave workers, and to prevent any possibility of the employers providing work for the people." A no less fervent colleague said more succinctly, "The lash of the dictator will be felt."[3] The Roosevelt revolution succeeded only because the deprived, supported by the socially concerned, became the electoral majority in the 1930s. What is important to remember as a lesson from those distant years is the number and unyielding opposition of those whose comfort was invaded or seemingly threatened.

In the half century and more since the New Deal the position of the contented has been greatly strengthened, and very specifically, by the measures then so vehemently resisted. These protective programs for the aged, the ill, the farmers and the depositors in financial institutions have already been adequately detailed.

One of the still-acknowledged threats to contentment is inflation. Unlike the effect of declining output and unemployment, its effect is felt across the full spectrum of the economy, and it thus threatens a considerable proportion of the contented, especially those who live on fixed incomes or investment return and those with money to lend. In the age of contentment the prevention of in-

3. The two spokesmen were, respectively, Representatives John Taber and Daniel Reed. They are quoted in Arthur M. Schlesinger, Jr., *The Coming of the New Deal*, vol. 2 of *The Age of Roosevelt* (Boston: Houghton Mifflin, 1958), p. 311.

flation has therefore, plausibly and predictably, become a special concern, although that fact is little remarked.

The adverse effect of recession, on the other hand, is more limited and specific. The unemployment it produces is the primary affliction, but that is something that can be ignored by those not so affected. In the recession of the 1990s, although some millions exhausted their unemployment benefits and coverage had been greatly narrowed by the movement of workers from larger industry into small service enterprises, the pain from unemployment was for a long time not much discussed. The role of interest rates in preventing inflation, in contrast, remained central to all reputable economic discussion.

However intervention by the state may be condemned in the age of contentment, it has been relatively comprehensive when the interests of the contented are involved and relatively limited when the problems are those of the poor. In consequence, one may reasonably conclude that a recession or depression is much less likely to trigger redemptive government action than in the past. Intervention to provide employment and alleviate enhanced poverty and suffering is far less likely than hitherto. The contented electoral majority is or has been made relatively secure; it can watch the adversity elsewhere with sympathy but with no strong call for corrective measures. The recession of the early 1990s was a demonstration of the point. Proposals for compensatory action and mitigation of the newly inflicted hardship were for many months sketchy in the extreme and for long won little backing from either political party. The suffering, physical and psychic, was not wholly denied, but it was deemed to be caused by a normal and self-correcting aspect of the system, and from this came the promise of a prompt recovery. In an interesting recapture of the 1930s, the only declared therapy to relieve the hardship became oratory — the promise from Washington that the recession, however disagreeable for those affected, would be shallow and short. Joseph Schumpeter's view of recession and depression as therapeutic was not quite revived; instead, the yet more ancient view of the inevitability and automaticity of the cyclical process was substituted. This became the consensus; the contented were still in control.

Recessions do not come to an end in any easily predictable way, but there are, with time, outside influences that support a return to better economic conditions. Inventories are exhausted and must be replaced. The fears of consumers dull; those who are still solvent return to the dealers and the stores. Most important is the distinctive nature of the financial mind; this rather remarkable manifestation of human intelligence is characterized by a very short memory span. In consequence, the recollection of the economic effects of past disaster that has occurred because of past errors of optimism eventually dissolves. In its place comes a new confidence in the unique and extraordinary genius of a new generation; the impression of such genius is always held most strongly by the favored individuals of themselves. Usually there will be some variant in the speculative object or emphasis — as in the past, enthusiasm moving from program trading in securities to commodity futures, to stock options, to junk bonds, to urban real estate, to art. The enduring fact is, to repeat, the delusion of the financial mind along with the popular illusion, in spite of evidence strongly to the contrary, that association with large sums of money denotes economic insight. This insight is regularly ascribed to the greatest of bankers and is known to survive until the day when a sizable provision for loan losses is announced and impressive error must, in effect, be conceded.

Thus the chance is that recessions and the causative speculation will continue to be self-corrective just as error continues, with time, to subsume error. But neither can the possibility of enduring recession or depression be ruled out. Of some things we do not know.

A higher probability for the American economy is more gradual but more definitive stasis. This is already well under way as American manufacturing industry and the economy generally concede to the superior economic performance of other nations, principally Japan, Germany and the countries on the Pacific Rim. Important in this process are macroeconomic policies, those involving capital investment in particular. In the United States such policies are, as already noted, oriented to contentment, whereas in the economically more aggressive countries they serve business investment much more positively. There the military establishments also make a far lower claim on capital and highly qualified manpower, and, over all, there are attitudes and policies that serve aspiration as opposed to contentment. The plausible economic future for the United States, within the narrow limits that economic prediction allows — a limitation always to be stressed — is one of sadly deficient and erratic performance. Whether its effect will be severe enough to invade the basic contentment cannot be told.

14

The Reckoning, II

T HE TWO REMAINING THREATS to the age of contentment are unpopular military action and a revolt, in whatever form, of the underclass.

The independent power of the military in the United States has been sufficiently stressed, as also its alliance with and service to the community of the contented. Military expenditure, as we have seen, rewards a substantial and politically influential sector of that community; those who are put at risk or discomfort by military service come extensively from the economically less favored and some from the underclass. Their service, though described and praised as that of volunteers, is largely, though of course not universally, compelled by the alternative deprivation from which it is an escape.

Almost any military venture receives strong popular approval in the short run; the citizenry rallies to the flag and to the forces engaged in combat. The strategy and technology of the new war evoke admiration and applause. This reaction is related not to economics or politics but more deeply to anthropology. As in ancient times, when the drums sound in the distant forest, there is an assured tribal response. It is the rallying beat of the drums, not the virtue of the cause, that is the vital mobilizing force.

But this does not last. It did not as regards the minor adventures in Grenada and Panama, nor as regards the war with Iraq and Saddam Hussein. The effect of more widespread wars has been almost uniformly adverse.

World War I, although it evoked the most powerful of patriotic responses at the time, has passed into history largely as a mindless and pointless slaughter. The party victoriously in power at the time, the Democrats, was rewarded in 1920 with a stern defeat at the polls. World War II, made inescapable by Japanese and German initiation or declaration of war, has survived with better reputation. However, the Korean and Vietnam wars, both greatly celebrated in their early months, ended with eventual rejection of the wars themselves and of the administrations responsible. In the longer run, it cannot be doubted, serious war deeply disturbs the political economy of contentment.

The military power in its substantial strength could be a threat to the culture of contentment in the future. The Vietnam war, it cannot be doubted, strongly challenged the contemporary attitudes of the contented and sent hundreds of thousands into the streets in protest. A serious military conflict, certainly one that enforced general participation and brought combat or destruction to the

American continent, would have a similar and undoubtedly even stronger effect. This would then extend on to the economic and social context that nurtures and defends contentment and would bring a serious reappraisal and rejection thereof. So, no doubt, would any extended participation in some lesser conflict in the Americas or abroad. It is a possibility on which all who see the United States in the emergent role of world police officer might reflect.

Set against this danger, however, are the considerable forces from within the community and polity of contentment that recognize the risks from major military adventure or are otherwise averse and that thus act as a restraining hand. This salutary sense of caution, it is well known, extends into the military establishment itself. And with the near-elimination of Communism there is also the diminished role of the war-nurturing anti-Communist paranoia among the contented. This, in turn, has lessened the seeming need for military deployment and action against areas of presumed (if improbable) Communist expansion.

On the other hand, the military establishment in the United States, as already seen, operates out of an internal power of its own. This means, with much else, that a plausible enemy is not wholly necessary. As this is written, Communism has collapsed; the Cold War has ended; dramatic further agreements were reached with the former Soviet Union reducing the deployment of nuclear weaponry. The military budget, nonetheless, has remained relatively unaffected. Here, to repeat, is proof of the autonomous power of the military.

It is in the nature of war, as Clausewitz observed, that its only certainty is uncertainty. The future effect of the military power on the polity of contentment cannot be foreseen. The danger can be cited but not assessed. Forecast becomes speculation. If one invokes the broad principle that the future will be much like the past, the military power will continue. So, almost certainly, will minor and seemingly safe wars. (It was Saddam Hussein's distinctive service to show that the threat of Communism was not the only reason for armed intervention.) Beyond that one cannot go.

A clearer threat to contentment comes from those who are left outside its comfort — from the underclass in the urban slums to which it has been extensively consigned.

The members of the underclass, it has been noticed, do not live in a homogeneous sense of adversity. By all the accepted standards of contentment, life in the inner city is poor, mean and on frequent occasion dangerous. There is escape into drugs, alcohol and violence. But by comparison with life in the communities or countries whence many of their inhabitants have come — from Mexico, Central America and Haiti to the United States, as from Turkey and North Africa to Western Europe — it is an improvement. However little, there is more; for some there is release from more forthright political and economic repression. However insecure the new life and its surroundings, this insecurity is viewed as less than the dangers of war and civil conflict once experienced. Better and safer life in the barrios of Los Angeles than existence in El Salvador or Nicaragua. And, as we have seen, this sense of improvement is not confined to those crossing national boundaries. It was once strongly felt by those in the United States who left the politically and socially dismal existence of the sharecropper South or the Appalachian valleys for the urban slums. Some of the enhanced modern perception of an underclass, as already observed, has resulted from its having become visible in the cities. On the cotton plantations of the Mississippi Delta, in the adjacent hills or in the valleys of the Appalachians it was not.

Yet the possibility of an underclass revolt, deeply disturbing to contentment, exists and grows stronger. There have been outbreaks in the past, notably the major inner-city riots in the latter 1960s, and there are several factors that might lead to a repetition.

In particular, it has been made clear, tranquillity has depended on the comparison with previous discomfort. With time, that comparison fades, and also with time the past promise of escape from relative privation — of upward movement — diminishes. This especially could be the consequence of a slowing or shrinking economy and even more of a prolonged recession or depression. The successive waves of workers who served the Detroit auto factories and body shops — the refugees from the adjacent farmlands of Michigan and Ontario and later the poor whites from Appalachia — went up and on. Many of those who came from the South to replace them are now stalled in endemic unemployment. No one should be surprised if this should, someday, breed a violent reaction. It has always been one of the high tenets of comfort that the uncomfortable accept peacefully, even gladly, their fate. Such a belief today may be suddenly and surprisingly disproved.

What is, perhaps, most certain is the reaction of the community of contentment to the miseries and violence of the urban slums and the probable reaction if the violence becomes more extreme. Aiding prediction, as ever, is the fact that the future, in some measure, is already here.

The first development, one we can already see, is resort by the contented in the larger cities to a laager mentality — the hiring of personal, neighborhood or apartment security guards or the escape to presumptively safe suburbs. In Manila in the Philippines affluent urban enclaves — the golden ghettos — are distributed over that poverty-ridden metropolis, each with its own impenetrable fence and stern security force. In less formal fashion, something of the same can now be seen in the modern American city, and this development could be, and one can doubtless say will be, greatly extended. In contrast with steps to tackle and ameliorate the economic and social forces shaping the despair and violence of the slums, such a protective remedy has an appealing element of immediacy and practicality: seemingly far better and surer the effect of outlays for security guards than the more distant hope from some rehabilitative expenditure in the inner city.

The second reaction is the likelihood, indeed near certainty, of what will happen if urban discontent, crime and violence increase: this will be attributed not to the social situation but to the inferior, even criminal, disposition of the people involved. Such is already the case. A major answer to crime, disaffection and disorder in the central cities is now a call for heavier law enforcement, including a more extensive use of the death penalty and more facilities for detention. No other current situation produces such inflammatory rhetoric. This mood, in the event of still worse violence, could, in turn, lead readily to armed repression, first by the local police, then by military force — the National Guard. The obvious fact that people of comfortable circumstance live peacefully together and those afflicted by poverty do not goes largely unnoticed. Or, if noticed, it is not discussed amidst the clamor for a clampdown on what seems an intrinsically ill-behaved and violent citizenry. Were one permitted one confident prediction, it would be of the likelihood of an increasingly oppressive authority in areas of urban desolation.

A final point must be emphasized. Recession and depression made worse by long-run economic desuetude, the danger implicit in an autonomous military power and growing unrest in the urban slums caused by worsening deprivation and hopelessness have been cited as separate prospects. All could, in fact, come together. A deep recession could cause stronger discontent in the areas of urban disaster in the aftermath of some military misadventure in which, in the nature of the modern armed forces, the unfortunate were disproportionately engaged. This could, indeed, be at grave cost to contentment. But, as sufficiently established, it is not in the nature of contentment that such eventualities, however persuasively described, be other than ignored. Contentment sets aside that which, in the longer view, disturbs contentment; it holds firmly to the thought that the long run may never come.

15

Requiem

B OOKS OF THIS GENRE are expected to have a happy
ending. With awareness of what is wrong, the corrective forces of democracy are set in motion. And
perhaps they would be now were they in a full democracy — one that embraced the interests and votes of all
the citizens. Those now outside the contented majority
would rally, or, more precisely, could be rallied, to their
own interest and therewith to the larger and safer public
interest. Alas, however, we speak here of a democracy of
those with the least sense of urgency to correct what is
wrong, the best insulation through short-run comfort
from what could go wrong.

There is special occasion here for sadness — for a sad
ending — for what is needed to save and protect, to ensure
against suffering and further unpleasant consequence, is
not in any way obscure. Nor would the resulting action
be disagreeable. There would be a challenge to the present
mood of contentment with its angry resentment of any
intrusion, but, in the longer run, the general feeling of
security in well-being would be deepened. Basic to this

greater long-run security is the nature of the modern industrial economy.

In the decades since World War II in the United States, in Western Europe and Japan, and elsewhere in the countries on the Pacific Rim, the modern economy with its admixture of market incentives and public intervention has shown phenomenal strength. Nor can it be supposed that this reflects the uniquely wise guidance of those charged with its governance. The marvel of the modern mixed economy is its potential internal strength and its resulting ability, on frequent occasion, to surmount the inadequacy, error, indifference or grave ignorance of those assumed to be responsible for its performance.

But not entirely. As the case of the American economy reveals, if negligent or perverse policy is powerful enough, the result can be visibly adverse. So it has been in these last years. But this does not mean that there is anything especially subtle about what would be required for remedy — for improvement. Further invasion of short-run contentment is inevitable; the nature of that invasion and of the remedy that would result is supremely evident. Economists regularly invoke the subtle, even incomprehensible, to imply or demonstrate a deeper competence and wisdom or to cover a grave difficulty that conveniently defies corrective action. No one should be misled.

The central requirement cannot be escaped: almost every action that would remedy and reassure involves the relationship between the citizen and the state. In the

Communist world in the long years before collapse all concessions to the market were resisted as concessions to capitalism; they were, to remind, inconsistent with the accepted principles of socialism. It was, however, almost certainly by such concessions, especially in the diverse world of consumer goods and services and agriculture — economic activity beyond the reach and competence of the command system — that Communism *cum* socialism might have been saved. In a perverse way, the same is now true of modern capitalism. Although intervention by the state on a wide and varied front once saved capitalism, there is now a resistance to the state action that is necessary to ensure an economically successful and socially tranquil future. The dialectic of the modern capitalist, or more precisely the modern mixed, economy all but exclusively involves the role of government. In the dialectic this is extensively ideological; in everyday manifestation it is highly pragmatic. And, to repeat, no subtlety conceals the needed attitude and action.

But on nothing has the culture of contentment been so successful as in shaping the accepted attitude toward the state. In some areas already emphasized — the armed services, the procurement of highly technical weaponry — the state's performance is, to be sure, approved. In the conduct of foreign policy, real and rhetorical, the provision of Social Security and the rescue of failing financial institutions, its adequacy is assumed. Where, however, regulation to forestall the socially damaging or self-destructive tendencies of the system or to rescue the poor is involved, state action is held to be deeply inadequate and seriously counterproductive. The public servants thus employed are thought to be bureaucratic, feckless, incompetent, on occasion self-seeking or corrupt and certainly ineffective. And there is, alas, the possibility that such inadequacy follows, in some measure, from this conditioned attitude. If public servants are widely publicized as inept and incompetent, so, quite possibly, some of them become. The people who serve well are those who are hailed for serving well. This being as it may be, the first need in correcting the current situation is to agree that the state's performance is equally eminent and necessary, whether it is for the contented or for the excluded. The present distinctions as to public competence all too obviously serve the purposes of short-run escape.

The required change in policy begins with the overall or macroeconomic performance of the economy. That the economy needs public guidance is wholly agreed; this is the legacy of the great revolution wrought by John Maynard Keynes. No longer can economic stability, growth, employment and the prevention of inflation be left to God and laissez faire. But the required regulation is now all but exclusively accomplished by the manipulation of interest rates to control the flow of demand coming from business investment and consumer borrowing. Lower interest rates enhance production and employment; higher rates prevent inflation.

The inescapable need is that macroeconomic regulation now be exercised in substantial measure through the public budget, not through monetary policy as at present, for this is deeply damaging to longer-run investment and industrial performance. When inflation threatens, the primary curb should not be on borrowing for productive investment but on private consumption by means of taxation and, where not socially damaging, deferred public expenditure. Investment and resulting gains in industrial productivity would not thus be put at risk in the interests of price stability. This was fully accepted in the years of American economic eminence following World War II;[1] nothing now runs more sharply against the comfortable commitment against tax increases. Or against the rentier reward from high interest rates.

In a time of economic recession such as that of the early 1990s, there is a strong case not only for low interest rates but also for increased public expenditure, especially on roads, bridges, airports and other civic needs, and on unemployment compensation and welfare payments, all to employ or protect the unemployed and those otherwise adversely affected.

But there is here a conflict with the tenets of the age of contentment: it is not the comfortable who would thus be aided. And lurking also is the eventual tax effect. During the 1980s, the burgeoning years of contentment, there

1. Lyndon Johnson was sharply criticized in the 1960s for a delay in raising taxes to meet the cost of the Vietnam war, and this delay was much cited as a cause of the later inflation.

was the large continuing deficit in the federal budget. Though a topic for voluble discourse, it was less of a threat to the contented than the taxes that would have reduced it. In the ensuing recession a deliberate addition to the deficit, a benefit primarily for those outside the community of contentment and one which might later renew the call for higher levies on those inside, was strongly resisted.

The controlling role of taxation continues. The only effective design for diminishing the income inequality inherent in capitalism is the progressive income tax. Nothing in the age of contentment has contributed so strongly to income inequality as the reduction of taxes on the rich; nothing, as has been said, so contributes to social tranquillity as some screams of anguish from the very affluent. That taxes should now be used to reduce inequality is, however, clearly outside the realm of comfortable thought. Here the collision between wise social action and the culture of contentment is most apparent.

Government action is also inescapable as regards the deeply inherent and self-destructive tendencies of the economic system. The dismal consequences, not least for those involved, of the great speculative (and frequently larcenous) activity of the 1980s are wonderfully evident. These could have been averted by timely and responsible regulatory action. Had the speculative excesses of the savings and loan associations and also the commercial banks been prevented by scrupulous regulation — something that was both possible and practical — there would have been no need for the subsequent enormous and infinitely more costly intervention to bail those institutions out. Michael Milken, the architect of the junk-bond explosion, could have been far more inexpensively restrained by earlier regulation than by later charges of criminal action. He would thus also have been spared the varied discomforts and indignities of a minimum-security gaol.

The mergers and acquisitions mania of the 1980s could have been halted in its early stages by legislation requiring hearings and a waiting period to assess the virtue of any large substitution of debt for equity — the universal feature of corporate raiding, other mergers and leveraged buyouts. For numerous corporations the restraining effect of debt and interest payments on investment and productivity and the many noted bankruptcies would thus have been avoided at small cost.

The present and devastated position of the socially assisted underclass has been identified as the most serious social problem of the time, as it is also the greatest threat to long-run peace and civility.

Life in the great cities in general could be improved, and only will be improved, by public action — by better schools with better-paid teachers, by strong, well-financed welfare services, by counseling on drug addiction, by employment training, by public investment in the housing that in no industrial country is provided for the poor by private enterprise, by adequately supported health care, recreational facilities, libraries and police. The question once again, much accommodating rhetoric to the contrary, is not what can be done but what will be paid. The case of education calls for a special word. Its importance is recognized; that educational shortcomings have weakened the American economic position is widely discussed. There has been much talk of educational reform; President George Bush has sought to have himself called the Education President; absent only has been the willingness to appropriate and spend public funds, especially those on the schools in the central cities. Without this willingness no significant educational improvement can be expected. Here there is the predictable bar to effective action when the overriding issues of public cost and possible taxation are encountered.[2]

Finally, there is the autonomous military power. Its now-vast claim on public funds — and taxation — and its further claim on scarce capital and manpower have been adequately noted, as has its contribution to economic decline in the United States as compared with Germany and Japan, which have not been so burdened. Following the collapse of Communism and the end of the Cold War, there seemed, for a moment, hope of change in this area. There was, as earlier indicated, brief reference to a peace

2. There is error, as ever, in undue generalization as to the quality of American education. In better-situated suburbs it can be excellent. And the universities, in particular the publicly financed state universities in which, in the main, the offspring of the contented are enrolled, are, not surprisingly, the best in the world.

dividend — not a capital saving from a major reduction in military expenditure but a dividend.

Not recognized, however, are the two vital factors already mentioned. The autonomous power of the military establishment is substantially independent of the existence of an enemy; its power is self-sustaining. And, in any case, a relatively minor enemy such as Saddam Hussein or even Manuel Noriega is wholly serviceable. With the war in the Gulf mention of a peace dividend largely disappeared. The resources now going to the military establishment, those devoted to such dubious weaponry as Star Wars and the Stealth bomber, would, if available, work a minor revolution in education and be a source of salvation and tranquillity in the central cities. But no one should doubt the formidable opposition of the autonomous military power as it stands in the way.

In an earlier chapter I raised the possibility that, in the future, near or far, a candidate for the American presidency will emerge who is committed to the human needs and remedies briefly just mentioned. And perhaps, if the electorate is enlarged to include the economically and socially now-disenfranchised, he or she will succeed and bring along a favoring majority in the Congress. As I said before, the prospect is not bright.

In the past, writers, on taking pen, have assumed that from the power of their talented prose must proceed the remedial action. No one would be more delighted than I were there similar hope from the present offering. Alas, however, there is not. Perhaps as a slight, not wholly inconsequential service, it can be said that we have here had the chance to see and in some small measure to understand the present discontent and dissonance and the not inconsiderable likelihood of an eventual shock to the contentment that is the cause.

Index

Acid rain, logic of inaction on, 20–21

Acquisitions, corporate
adverse effects of, 58, 59
and 1990s recession, 157
ways of halting, 180
See also Corporate raiding

Advertising, television, and consumer sovereignty, 134

AFDC (Aid to Families with Dependent Children), Murray on, 105–7

Afghanistan, U.S. intervention in, 140

African-Americans. See Blacks

Agriculture. See Farmers

AID programs, 113, 117

Airlines, financial devastation of, 57–58

American Liberty League, 160

Angola, U.S. intervention in, 140

Anthropology
and reaction to war, 166–67
in study of political economy of contentment, 11–12
and Veblen's critique, 81

Aspin, Les, 131n

Austria
outside workers in, 34–36
and politics of contentment, 152–53
wages policy in, 87–88

Bank(s), and real estate boom, 59–61

Bank failures
and function of government, 14, 48–49, 61, 83, 122–23
and 1990s recession, 157–58
and real estate boom, 60–61
regulation as preventing, 179–80

Batra, Dr. Raui, 159n

Berle, Adolf, 5, 54n

Bilderberg convocation, 116

Blacks
in armed forces, 131
post-WWII migration of, 39
in underclass, 31

Bloomingdale's, 57

Boesky, Ivan, 103

Britain
and free trade, 80
Labourites in, 19, 152
Lloyd George's welfare measures in, 3
politics of contentment in, 151–52
underclass disorder in, 38

Budget deficits. See Deficit, budget

Bulgaria, overthrow of Communism in, 8–9. See also Eastern Europe

Bureaucracy
military as, 71
private vs. public, 66–67, 77

Bureaucracy (*cont.*)
 and private sector, 72–77, 134
 and public service, 70–72
Burlington Industries, 57n
Burnham, James, 54n
Burrough, Bryan, 54n
Bush, George, and Bush administration
 on class-division absence, 30
 and education, 181
 and foreign policy, 114
 Panama attacked by, 140
 and Persian Gulf war, 141–42
 as responsive to contented majority, 18, 22, 26
 and Roosevelt on expenditure reduction, 4
 taxes opposed by, 48, 49–50
Buyouts, leveraged
 of airlines, 57–58
 and debt-for-equity regulation, 59, 180
 and Gilder on wealth, 103
 and 1990s recession, 157
Buyouts by management, 56–59

Campeau, Robert, 57
Canada
 and 1990s recession, 157
 and politics of contentment, 152
 poverty in vs. in U.S., 107
Capitalism
 and Adam Smith, 99
 British welfare measures as saving, 3
 and contentment of many, 10
 and corporate management, 53–56
 economics in service to, 80
 instability of, 83–85
 as precondition of Communism, 125, 140
 progressive income tax needed with, 179
 self-destructiveness of, 53, 59
 state (U.S.) intervention as saving, 176

 and public programs, 52
 and Roosevelt, 6
 and underclass, 36, 37
Carey, Henry, 80
Central bank, 43, 89, 90, 91, 92
China, Communist, 24
Classical economists, 3
Classless society, mythology of, 30
Clausewitz, Carl von, 169
Communism
 collapse of, 8–9, 142, 143, 181
 as internal threat in U.S., 124–25
 and legislator's commitments, 125, 137
 market resisted by, 176
 and military establishment or expenditures, 24, 25, 48, 123–26, 127, 133, 137, 138–41, 142–43, 168
 See also Socialism
Communist China, 24
Compensation
 for executives, 55–56, 74
 and type of work, 32–33
Competition. *See* Market
Congress, U.S.
 and military, 137
 and S&L regulation, 63
Consumers' goods economy, and socialism, 7–8
Consumer sovereignty, 133–35
Contented individuals and communities
 accommodation of belief in service of, 2–3, 10, 81–82
 Communist elites as, 9
 short-sighted responses of, 6–7, 82–83
 U.S. majority of voters as, 10
Contented majority. *See* Culture of contentment
Coolidge, Calvin, 92, 155
Corporate raiding, 56–59
 and debt-for-equity regulation, 59, 180
 and Gilder on wealth, 103

Index

Corporation(s)
  Adam Smith averse to, 99–100
  and bureaucracy, 72–77
  management power in, 53–56
  as organization, 66 (see also
    Organization)
  Council on Foreign Relations, 115,
    115n
Cranston, Alan, 137
Crime, in inner cities, 38
Culture of contentment (contented
    majority), 15, 16–17
  anthropology in study of, 11–12
  definition of, 15–16
  dissent from, 17, 19
  future change in, 155, 156–57
    through economic disaster,
      157–65
    hope for lacking, 11–12, 182–83
    and 1920s comparison, 155–56
    through underclass revolt,
      170–73
    through unpopular military
      action, 166–69
  government as reflecting, 18, 22,
    26, 28, 50
  and government's proper func-
    tion, 14–15, 22–26, 48–49,
    83, 122–23, 176–77
  income differences tolerated,
    26–27, 179
  and inflation, 92
  and interest rates, 43, 92
  military approved by, 23–25, 48,
    127
  and military service, 127–31,
    141
  moral smugness of, 18–20
  and organizational culture, 66–
    70, 76
  and politics, 144 (see also Poli-
    tics of contentment)
  and private vs. public bureauc-
    racy, 66–67, 77
  remedies for faults of, 174–75
    and macroeconomic policy,
      177–79

  and military expenditures,
    181–82
  and recognition of value of
    government, 176–77
  and speculative excesses, 179–
    80
  and underclass, 180–81
  short-sightedness of, 20–22, 94,
    173
  and taxes, 17, 44, 178–79 (see
    also Taxes)
  and underclass, 29, 31, 32, 40–
    41
  See also Contented individuals
    and communities
Currie, Lauchlin, 5
Czechoslovakia, overthrow of
  Communism in, 8–9. See
  also Eastern Europe

Defense establishment. See Mili-
    tary establishment and ex-
    penditures
Deficit, budget, 87
  and interest charges, 93
  and logic of inaction on, 22
  and 1990s recession, 157–58
  and tax policy, 49, 179
Democracy
  and authority of military, 138
  and beliefs of contented, 10
  corrective capacity of, 154, 174
  and culture of contentment, 15,
    154–55, 174
  and dissenters, 19
  and economic development–
    public participation relation,
    8
  and nonvoters, 15, 150–51, 153
  and socially excluded groups,
    151
  U.S. government as responsive
    to electoral majority, 18, 22,
    26, 28, 50
Democratic Party, 145–46, 148–49
  twenty years of dominance by,
    156

Democratic Party (*cont.*)
  wars fought under, 149–50
  and World War I, 167
DeMott, Benjamin, 30n
Depression, 84
  action against, 85–86
  causes of, 85
  current fear of, 159–60
  and government intervention, 162
  and instability of capitalism, 83
  and monetary policy, 95
  Schumpeter's view on, 163
  and underclass revolt, 170, 172–73
  See also Great Depression;
    Recession
Deregulation
  of airlines, 57–58
  and S&Ls, 62, 63
  and Adam Smith, 100
Distribution of income. *See* Income distribution in U.S.
Downey, Thomas J., 137
Drug dealing, in inner cities, 38
Dukakis, Michael, 149

Eastern Airlines, 58
Eastern Europe
  collapse of Communism in, 7–10, 142, 143
  military defense against, 24
  and socialism as screen, 151
  and threat of Communism, 125
  Warsaw Pact, 139, 139n
  Western help needed by, 121
East Germany, overthrow of Communism in, 8–9. *See also*
  Eastern Europe
Economics
  as accommodation, 78–82, 95, 96–98
  and Adam Smith, 98–101, 107
  and Gilder, 101–3
  and Laffer, 103–5
  and laissez faire, 79, 82–83
  and monetary policy, 88–93, 95–96 (*see also* Monetary policy)

  supply-side, 108
  and consumer sovereignty or profit maximization, 133–35
  fiscal policy, 43–45, 86–87
  and taxes, 42–43 (*see also* Taxes)
Economists
  classical, 3 (*see also* Laissez faire)
  and New Deal measures, 4–5
Education, 181, 181n
  in burden of government, 25–26
  and taxation, 45
Eisenhower, Dwight D., 156
Elderly, in contented majority, 16
El Salvador, U.S. intervention in, 140
Entrepreneurs
  and corporate bureaucracy, 75–76
  economists as affirming, 2–3
Equity
  and economic function, 158–59
  and market, 52
  and taxes, 179
Exchange rate, and interest rate, 93
Executive compensation, 55–56
  and market discipline, 74

Farmers
  Reagan support of, 122
  satisfaction of, 16
  and socialism, 7
Federal Reserve Board, 158
Federal Reserve System, 43, 90, 91
Federated Department Stores, 57
Fernandez, Richard L., 129n, 130n
Fiscal policy, 86–87
  and political neutrality, 43–45
  See also Keynes, John Maynard;
    Taxes
Food stamps, 44
  Murray on, 105–7
Forbes magazine, 55n
Ford, Gerald, 156
Foreign policy
  and American economic power, 113, 117–21

Index

Foreign policy (*cont.*)
  and American military power,
    117–18, 120–21, 123, 126
  and democracy of contentment,
    155
  and diplomats as contented,
    114–16
  rewards for practice of, 111–13
  and state's performance, 176
  and threat from unpopular military action, 166–69
  and trade deficit, 94
  undemanding character of, 109–11
  and world police role, 168
  See also Communism
Fortune magazine, 55n
France
  of Louis XV and XVI, 2
  outside workers in, 34–36
  and politics of contentment,
    152–53
  underclass disorder in, 38
Freedom of expression, and economic development, 8
Free trade
  Adam Smith for, 99
  for Britain, 80
Friedman, Benjamin, 56n
Friedman, Milton, 89

General Motors Corporation, 73
Germany
  and civilian industry, 119–20
  outside workers in, 34–36
  in Persian Gulf war, 120–21
  and politics of contentment,
    152–53
  post-WWII attitude of, 119
  poverty in vs. in U.S., 107
  superior economic performance
    of, 164
  wages policy in, 87–88
  See also East Germany
Gilded Age, 80
Gilder, George, 27n, 101–3, 101n,
    102n
Global warming, and logic of inaction on, 21

Golden ghettos, 171
Golden parachutes, 55
Government (U.S.)
  bureaucracy of, 66–67, 70–71,
    76–77
  and capitalist instability, 83–86
  conception of as burden, 22–23,
    46, 147
  fiscal policy used by, 43–45, 86–
    87
  and intervention in recession or
    depression, 162
  military department heads, 136
  monetary policy used by, 43,
    88–93, 95–96 (*see also* Monetary policy)
  proper function of, 14–15, 22–
    26, 48–49, 61, 83, 122–23,
    176–77 (*see also* Laissez
    faire)
  Reagan's criticism of, 122–23
  recognition of need for, 176–
    77
  as representative of electoral
    majority, 18, 22, 26, 28, 50
  services from, 1, 44–47, 49, 178
  wage and price controls used by,
    87–88
Great Depression, 3–4, 155–56
  fear of repeat of, 159
  and government function, 83
  and hopeful rhetoric, 85
  and stock market crash, 1
Greider, William, 107n
Grenada, U.S. invasion of, 139–40,
    149, 167

Health care
  in burden of government, 25–
    26
  contented majority for, 122
  and rich vs. poor, 46
Helyar, John, 55n
Henderson, Leon, 5
Highways, and logic of inaction
  on, 21
Hoover, Herbert, 155
Hoover, J. Edgar, 124

Index

Housing
in burden of government, 25–26
public subsidy of, 44
Hungary, overthrow of Communism in, 8–9. *See also* Eastern Europe
Hussein, Saddam, 169, 182. *See also* Persian Gulf war

Immigration, to U.S., 37
Income distribution in U.S., 13–14
and culture of contentment, 26–27, 179
and economic function, 158–59
and executive compensation, 55–56
and market, 52
and taxes, 14n
Inflation
action against, 86
causes of, 84
contented majority's fear of, 92
and fiscal policy, 86–87
and instability of capitalism, 83
and interest rates, 90–91, 93, 162, 177
proper policy for, 178
threat from, 161
Infrastructure of United States, and logic of inaction on, 21
Inner cities. *See* Poverty and the poor; Underclass, functional
Inside information, trading with, 58
Interest payments, income from, 92
Interest rates, 92, 177
and inflation, 90–91, 93, 162, 177
lack of concern for, 43, 92–93
and monetary policy, 90–91
and 1990s recession, 157–58
and trade deficit, 93
International Monetary Fund, 117
International trade, and logic of inaction on, 22
Iraq, war with. *See* Persian Gulf war

Italy
post-WWII attitude of, 119
south-to-north labor migration in, 34

Japan
and civilian industry, 119–20
economic strength of, 175
in Persian Gulf war, 120–21
post-WWII attitude of, 119
superior economic performance of, 164
wages policy in, 87–88
Johnson, Lyndon, 156, 178n
Junk bonds, 58
and Gilder on wealth, 103

Keating, Charles, 75
Kemmerer, Edwin W., 5
Kennedy, John F., 88, 156
Keynes, John Maynard, 42, 82–83, 87, 177
Kissinger, Henry, 156
Korean War
and Democratic Party, 149–50, 156
reaction to, 167

Laager mentality, 171
Labour Party, British, 152
Labour politicians, and "working" of democracy, 19
Laffer, Arthur, 103–5, 105n
Laissez faire, 20, 51
as accommodation, 79, 82–83, 96
and corporate raiding, 58
and market, 51–53
and 1980s real estate speculation, 61
self-destructiveness of, 53, 59
and S&L scandal, 61–64
Law enforcement, call for, 172
Lebanon, Marines sent into, 139
Leisure class
J. P. Morgan's defense of, 5–6
See also Veblen, Thorstein

Liberals
and community of contentment,
146
in defense against Communism,
24
and "working" of democracy, 19
Libya, air strike on, 139
List, Friedrich, 80
Lloyd George, David, 3

McCarthyism, 124
McNamara, Robert, 105n, 107n
Malthus, Thomas Robert, 3, 78–
79, 96
Management
buyouts by, 56–59
corporations controlled by, 53–56
Market, 51–52
Communists against, 176
and corporate bureaucracy, 76
and corporate personnel changes,
74
and corporate raiding, 58
and energy cost control, 88
inequities of, 52
and 1980s real estate speculation, 61
and public-service industries, 57
self-destructiveness of, 53, 59
and S&L scandal, 61–64
as totem, 134–35
Marshall Plan, 113, 117
Marx, Karl
on capitalism before Communism, 125
and convenient belief, 9
Mass transportation, and logic of
inaction on, 21
Means, Gardiner C., 5, 54n
Media (press)
as contented majority, 147
and Persian Gulf war, 142
Medicaid, Murray on, 105–7
Mental effort, attempts to avoid, 68
Mergers
adverse effects of, 58, 59
and 1990s recession, 157

ways of halting, 180
See also Corporate raiding
Migrant farm workers, 37
Military establishment and expenditures
and Adam Smith, 100
autonomous power of, 131–32,
133, 135–38, 168–69, 181–82
as averse to major adventure,
168
as bureaucracy, 71
and Communism, 24, 25, 48,
123–26, 127, 133, 137, 138–
41, 142–43, 168
contented majority's approval of,
23–25, 48, 127
contented majority's under- representation in, 127–31, 141
future of, 169
and Persian Gulf war, 141–42
and policies of foreign competi-
tors, 164
Reagan buildup of, 126–27
Reagan-Bush exercise of, 139–
40
and Reagan criticism of government, 122, 123
of U.S. vs. Germany/Japan, 119–
20
Military power (U.S.), and foreign
policy, 117–18, 120–21, 123,
126
Milken, Michael, 103, 180
Minority groups
in armed forces, 131
in underclass, 31
See also Blacks
Mobility, upward. *See* Upward mobility
Monetarism, 89–90
Monetary policy, 43, 88–93, 95–96
vs. monetarism, 89–90
need for lessened reliance on,
178
and 1990s recession, 157–58
and political-social neutrality,
43–45, 96

Monopoly, 52
Moral (just) desert, contented majority's welfare as, 18–20
Moral effects, of aid to poor vs. aid to wealthy, 14–15
Morgan, J. P., 5–6
Morgan Stanley and Company, 57n
Murray, Charles A., 105–7, 105n, 106n

New Deal, 4
and economists, 81
and Great Depression, 155–56
opposition to, 4–6
Nicaragua, U.S. intervention in, 140
Nicholas, Nicholas J., 55n
Nixon, Richard, 88, 156
Noonan, Peggy, 98n
Noriega, Manuel, 140, 182
Nuclear safety, concern over, 156
Nuclear war, and purposes of military, 139
Nye, Joseph S., 118n

Organization, 65–66
and bureaucracy, 70 (see also Bureaucracy)
common purpose in, 67–68
constraints on power of, 135–36
corporation as, 66 (see also Corporation)
independent thought surrendered to, 68
multiplication of personnel in, 69–70, 73–74
and private vs. public bureaucracy, 66–67, 77
problems delegated in, 68–69
Ozone layer, and logic of inaction on, 21

Pacific Rim
economic strength of, 175
superior economic performance of, 164
Pack, Spencer J., 99n
Palmer raids, 124

Panama, U.S. invasion of, 140, 149, 167
Pan American Airlines, 58
Pay. See Compensation
Peace dividend, 142, 182
Persian Gulf war (1991), 120–21, 141–42
and 1990s recession, 157
and peace dividend, 182
reaction toward, 167
as Republican war, 149
socioeconomic composition of forces at risk in, 131n
Phillips, Kevin, 27n, 98n
Physiocrats, 2
Poland, overthrow of Communism in, 8–9. See also Eastern Europe
Political economy of contentment
anthropology in study of, 11–12
and taxation, 44
Political experts, 148
Politics of contentment
in Britain, 151–52
and Democratic Party, 145–46, 148–50
and hope for candidate of the excluded, 153, 182
and media representatives, 147
and money, 146–47
and 1988 campaign, 149
and nonvoters, 15, 150–51, 153
and planning, 40
and Republican Party, 144–45
Poverty and the poor, 13
Gilder on, 102
incidence of, 13, 107
and moral effects of government aid, 14
Murray on, 105–7
need to minimize responsibility for, 97
in Ricardo's and Malthus's theory, 78–79
right to sleep under bridges or on street grates, 28
tax-supported services for, 44–46
and voting, 150–51

Poverty and the poor (*cont.*)
 See also Underclass, functional
Press. *See* Media
Price controls, 87–88
Profit maximization, 54–55, 76,
 133–34. *See also* Market
Proletarians, and culture of con-
 tentment, 16
Public agency, as organization, 66
Public participation in government
 and economic development, 8
 See also Democracy
Public services and expenditure
 and avoidance of depression, 1
 current need for, 178
 and inflation policy, 178
 and opposition to taxes, 46–47
 and rich vs. poor, 44–46, 46n, 49

Qaddafi, Muammar, 139

Reagan, Ronald, and Reagan
 administration, 28, 122, 123
 and Adam Smith, 98
 arms buildup of, 126–27
 and fiscal policy, 87
 good feeling from, 28
 military forays of, 139–40
 as responsive to contented majority, 18, 22, 26, 28, 122–23
 and Stockman interview, 107–8
 taxes opposed by, 27, 47–48, 49–
  50
Real estate speculation, of 1980s,
 59–61, 158
Recession, 84
 action against, 85–86
 adverse effect of, 162
 causes of, 85
 ending of, 163–64
 and government intervention,
  162
 and instability of capitalism, 83
 and monetarism, 90
 and monetary policy, 43, 88, 95
 and 1980s real estate speculation, 61
 of 1990s, 157–59, 162–63, 178

Schumpeter's view on, 163
 and underclass revolt, 170, 172–
  73
Regan, Donald, 63n
Reich, Robert B., 46n, 156n
Rentier class, 43, 96, 178
Republican Party, 144–45
 and military expenditures, 25
 and wars, 149
Ricardo, David, 3, 78–79, 96
RJR Nabisco, buyout of, 55n, 56,
 57n
Robbins, Lionel, 4–5, 5n
Rome after Trajan, 2
Roosevelt, Franklin D., 4
 and Depression, 155–56
 and J. P. Morgan, 6
 on State Department, 114
Roosevelt revolution, 6, 160–61
Ross, Steven J., 55n

Savings and loan scandal. *See* S&L
 scandal
Scandinavia
 outside workers in, 34–36
 and politics of contentment,
  152–53
 wages policy in, 87–88
Schlesinger, Arthur M., Jr., 6n,
 161n
Schulzinger, Robert D., 115n
Schumpeter, Joseph Alois, 4–5, 5n,
 75, 75n, 163
SDI (Star Wars), 127, 182
Self-interest, 50
 and management of corporations, 54–55
 profit maximization as, 54
 and social concern, 17
Short-sightedness
 of contented individuals and
  communities, 6–7, 82–83
 in culture of contentment, 20–
  22, 77, 94, 173
 in opposition to welfare programs, 52
 of Republican Party, 145
 and S&L scandal, 61–62

Index

S&L (savings and loan) scandal,
  61–64
  and function of government, 14,
    48–49
  and Keating, 75
  and 1990s recession, 157–58
  regulation as preventing, 179–
    80
Smith, Adam, 54, 80, 98–101,
  100n, 107
Social concern, 17
Socialism
  causes of failure of (in Soviet
    bloc), 7–10
  and culture of contentment,
    123
  faults hidden under, 151
  market resisted by, 176
  See also Communism
Social Security, 14
  attacks on, 160–61
  and bureaucracy, 70–71
  contented majority for, 23, 122
  and state's performance, 176
Soviet Union
  collapse of Communism and so-
    cialism in, 7–10, 142, 143
  military defense against, 24, 139
  and threat of Communism, 125
  Western help needed by, 121
Spencer, Herbert, 80, 96, 101
Star Wars, 127, 182
State. See Government
Stockman, David, 107–8
Stock market crash
  current unlikelihood of, 164
  1929 vs. 1987, 1
Strategic Defense Initiative (Star
  Wars), 127, 182
Sumner, William Graham, 80–81,
  81n, 101
Supply-side economics, 108
Survival of the fittest, 80–81
Switzerland
  outside workers in, 34–36
  and politics of contentment,
    152–53
  wages policy in, 87–88

Tariffs, U.S. and Germany served
  by, 80
Taxes
  Adam Smith on, 100
  and British politics, 152
  and budget deficit, 49
  and bureaucracy, 70, 71
  and contented majority, 17, 44,
    178–79
  and Democratic Party, 146
  in fiscal policy, 86–87
  and foreign aid, 120
  Gilder on, 102
  and income distribution, 14,
    14n
  and inflation policy, 178
  Laffer on, 103–5
  and management of economy,
    42–43
  and 1990s recession, 157–58
  opposition to, 46–47
  progressive, 52, 179
  and public services, 44–46, 46n,
    49
  and Reagan/Bush administra-
    tions, 27, 47–48, 49–50
  and Republican Party, 145
  and state or local services, 159
  tolerance of reduction for
    wealthy, 26–27, 42
Technostructure, 72n
Television advertising, and con-
  sumer sovereignty, 134
Thatcher, Margaret, 151–52
Three Mile Island accident, 156
Tolstoy, Leo, 67
Trade deficit, 93–94
Trade unions, and wage-cost con-
  trol, 88
Trickle-down theory, 108
Trilateral Commission, 116
Truman, Harry S., 149
Trump, Donald, 59
Tugwell, Rexford Guy, 5

Underclass, functional, 29, 30–32,
  and comparison with former sit-
    uations, 39–40, 169–70

Underclass, functional (*cont.*)
and contented majority, 29, 31, 32, 40–41
and distasteful work, 33–34
measures to help, 180–81
need to minimize responsibility for, 97
and outside workers in Western Europe, 34–36, 152–53
and political practicality, 146, 148
revolt of, 170–73
and taxation of contented, 44
threat from, 180
and U.S. employment requirements, 36–38
violence and discontent in lives of, 38–39, 40, 169
and voting, 39–40, 150–51
See also Poverty and the poor
Unemployment compensation
as depression barrier, 1
Murray on, 105–7
United Kingdom. *See* Britain
United States
economic strength of, 175
majority contentment in, 10 (*see also* Contented individuals and communities)
well-off group in, 13–15 (*see also* Culture of contentment)
See also Government
United States Steel Corporation, 73
Upward mobility
and resupply of lowly workers, 33–34
and underclass tranquillity, 170–71
USSR. *See* Soviet Union

Veblen, Thorstein, 81
Vietnam war, 24
and competence of military, 141
and Democratic Party, 149–50

ending of, 156
reaction to, 167
resistance to, 129, 167
and social composition of armed forces, 128–29
and tax delay/inflation, 178n

Wage and price controls, 87–88
Waligorski, Conrad P., 78
Wanniski, Jude, 103–4
Wars
reaction to, 166–67
See also specific wars
Warsaw Pact, 139, 139n. *See also* Eastern Europe
Wealth of Nations (Smith), 98
Welfare services and expenditures
and bureaucracy, 70, 71, 72
contented majority opposition to, 25–26
and Democratic Party, 146
Murray against, 105–7
See also Public services and expenditure
Western Europe
economic strength of, 175
and 1990s recession, 157
outside workers in, 34–36, 152–53
and politics of contentment, 152–53
White, Harry Dexter, 5
Work, 32–33
and underclass functions, 33–34
Worker's Compensation, Murray on, 105–7
World Bank, 117
World War I
and Democratic Party, 149
response to, 167
World War II
and Democratic Party, 149
reputation of, 167
and U.S. satisfaction, 118–19